THE BLUE DIAMOND SOULS

Calling in the Next Generation

BY
ZAPHERIA BELL &
THE BLUE DIAMOND SOULS

First published in 2020 by Zapheria Bell

© Zapheria Bell
The moral rights of the author have been asserted.
This book is a SpiritCast Network of Books

Author:

Bell, Zapheria

Title:

The Blue Diamond Souls; Calling In The Next Generation

ISBN:

979-8616967-794

Editor-in-chief: Cherise Lily Nana
Cover Design: Sarah Rose Graphic Design

Disclaimer:
The material in this publication is of the nature of general comment only, and does not represent professional advice. It is not intended to provide specific guidance for particular circumstances and it should not be relied on as the basis for any decision to take action or not take action on any matter which it covers. Readers should obtain professional advice where appropriate, before making any such decision. To the maximum extent permitted by law, the author and publisher disclaim all responsibility and liability to any person, arising directly or indirectly from any person taking or not taking action based on the information in this publication.

This book is deeply dedicated to
The Blue Diamond Souls.
It's an honour to be your voice.

ACKNOWLEDGEMENTS

First and foremost I would like to deeply honour and thank The Blue Diamond Souls for reminding me of our Sacred agreement, that I would stand up and be your voice at this time. Thank you for trusting me to share your words with the world.

Of course there are always people who have been monumental in guiding our lives. Personally it has been quite a journey for me to be in a place where not only I am open to channelling and writing a book like this, but also happy to stand by it in the world.

I would like to take a moment to thank some of the prominent people on that journey.

It goes without saying, yet I'm going to say it – first and foremost my thank you is directed towards my parents, who are sensational people who love and support me no matter what I do in the world. They stand by me 100% through all the ups and downs and they have shown me I can be and do anything I put my heart and mind to.

Mumma & Daddyo I love you to the moon and back and I thank you from the bottom of my heart for all that you are. Jennie-lee and Andre Van Gelder, you are both such an inspiration to me in my life. Thank you for giving me life.

I quite literally could not have written this book without the hours and hours of questions read to the Blue Diamond Souls if I didn't have the very patient and loving support of my partner Michael Mathew. Thank you for believing in this work, for tirelessly asking questions and talking directly with the Blue

Diamond Souls through me. Thank you for holding a loving and non-judgemental space during this entire process. Thank you for showing up over and over again for the BDS and for your dedication and relationship with them. Most of all, thank you for being my rock! Thank you for showing me love.

In 2013 there was a sliding doors moment in my life where I met a man who has journeyed from being my practitioner to my mentor, and has become my dearest friend and business partner. Dane Tomas you quite literally changed my life. It all started the day I met you and for that I am deeply grateful. Thank you for your consistent love and support. Thank you for showing me a friendship that feels like the most genuine of my life. Thank you for showing me who I truly am.

To my mentor, teacher and beloved friend Janine MaRae, where do I even start? For you, the thank you seems beyond words, and a feeling deep within my Womb that speaks to you for awakening in me something that you could see but I could not. The way you held me, something opened in me that now ripples out to the world and awakens many more. Thank you for starting the ripple that will move through generations to come. Thank you for awakening my Magick.

Dearest Bruce Lyon, you see something in me beyond what I can even see myself. My Soul is always grateful for the journey that moves beyond lifetimes, beyond dimensions, beyond space and time. Thank you for waking me up to see that there is more, that I am more. My Cancerian self feels the depth of your love and care for me and she is forever grateful. My Magick sees your Magick and promises to continue to meet you in the place beyond. Thank you for awakening my Soul.

CONTENTS

INTRODUCTION

Welcome to a book that is written from my Heart, Womb and Soul in the deepest hope and desire that it reaches out and touches the lives of those who are ready to receive it. For some it will deeply resonate, activate, inspire and provide you with powerful transmissions. For some it may seem a little far-fetched and unusual, maybe even triggering. If that's you, I would recommend you read what resonates and come back to the book at another time, as you will receive different messages from it at different times on your own evolutionary path. There are transmissions and codes deep in the text so if you are a "feeling" type of person, I would also suggest you open and allow your body to feel the work as you read it.

Throughout my life I've danced with opening up to being a channel and medium, and shutting it down, choosing to follow a more "normal" path. Mostly when I've shut it down it's been because of my own fears of what people would think of me. Would they think I am crazy?

This book is about to change all of that.

I'm stepping up to write a book which is mostly channelled content and share it with the world. No longer hiding, because now I see it's way bigger than me, and because I practise what I preach. It's time for all of us to stand up and bring our full Soul's gifts to the world. No more hiding as the world needs each and every one of us – hopefully this book with help you see that for yourself too.

Looking at the state of the world today, it's time that we move quickly. We need to stop hiding in the shadows of our own fears and bring all of our gifts forward.

This is no longer about me and my own small fears, it's about the Blue Diamond Souls and a Greater Consciousness that are here to create a shift in Humanity as we know it, and the time to share that is NOW!

At the time of writing Australia was burning. Some say it had been orchestrated by the Government? Trump had orchestrated the assassination of a Military leader so perhaps we are about to see either another World War or maybe this is the start of leaders killing off other leaders – the start of the inevitable demise of leadership as we know it.

At the time of publishing the world is in shut down!

Something has to drastically change, so maybe this is it?

No matter what you believe in, if we want to stay living on this Earth and not drive ourselves to extinction, we need to make a change, and quickly!

That's what the Blue Diamond Souls are here to show us.

This book is for you if:

-You're a parent to one of these Souls who wishes to understand them more.

-You and your partner would like to conceive one of these Souls, especially if you are struggling to conceive a child and wish to know how you can increase your chances.

-You are interested in knowing more about the rise of Humanity and how you can support.

I'm writing this book to give these Souls a voice and because they have asked me to, because it's part of my Soul's calling and because it's time!

You should know this is not something I have researched or learnt from others.

Everything I know about The Blue Diamond Souls, they have shared with me directly.

As you read through the book you will find the channelled content is in italics to make it easier for you to spot when the Blue Diamond Souls (BDS) are talking and when it's me. I have asked them to provide the content in language that is as easy to read and understand as possible. Other than editing grammar and removing double up words to make it easier to read, the content is in their own choice of words. At times their languaging can be a little unusual to read, but I have chosen to keep the integrity of their words and not change them. Whilst channelling them there is a very distinct feeling of the translation needing to come from a Soul language into words that we will understand.

Read it and take what resonates with you. Share with your friends and loved ones.

At the back you will find links to plenty of bonus content, including the full transcription of more than 18,000 words.

MY STORY

Why do I choose to tell you my story in a book that's not about me?

I feel it's important to understand the background of how I ended up here, writing this book.

During the 9 days leading in to writing this book I have been fasting; 2 days of juice, 7 days water and 2 days soups. Why? To ensure what I channel onto these pages is the coming through a clear conduit and not caught up in the low vibrations of the food most of us eat on a daily basis.

An only child and only grandchild, I grew up in a relaxed small beach town on the Northern Beaches of Australia.

A young single mum, my mum worked hard to ensure she could give me everything in the world a girl could want. A side effect of that was that I spent a lot of time with my grandparents, at different times living with them or at the very least going there often. To be honest, I thought it was pretty awesome to have all the attention of my grandparents and my mum. A few years later the final piece of the family puzzle landed as my Dad walked into our lives and made our little family complete.

Being a kid was great! Yet I also had many hidden demons that would come out as I grew up, beliefs and conditioning that started to impact who I was once I hit teenage years, but I will save those for another book.

I had a secret connection to other realms, which many children do – until adults shut it down and tell them they are wrong or don't believe their "silly stories"... I could see Faeries and thought it quite normal to chat to them and build them places to live in the garden. When our neighbour died, I thought it was normal to have conversations with her, and to know when she was in my house. I was never scared.

Yet I also did have the "scary" people come to my room. The ones I would try to hide from under the bed. They could talk to me too and I didn't know how to be selective about what I saw and heard, so eventually I thought it was better to just shut it all down and pretend I couldn't see or hear any of these other people in my room.

Until one day, when I met a man. (I know, it's always about a Man! :p)

He intrigued me, captured my interest and I was lost in a whirlwind romance at 18.

When I asked him, "Where are you from?", he just mysteriously pointed upwards. I knew there was something different about this man and I wanted to know more – so like the spontaneous 18-year-old that I was, within a week I moved out of my family home and moved in with him. Don't ask what my parents thought of that one!

From then everything changed path again. Everything I had closed down started to open up more than ever.

Suddenly everything seemed to make sense! Magick started to open up in my world and I finally felt like I found where I belonged. I started practising Wicca, Meditation, Astral Travel, studying Kabbalah, inner world theories and opening myself up to everything I could find.

My channel well and truly opened and I spent a lot of time channelling and writing; hearing, seeing and knowing things I hadn't read anywhere else. Life made sense. I was also doing Crystal Healing and hands-on healing and people were having big transformations on my table. Kundalini activations, which I didn't know what they were at the time so it was quite confronting and physical changes happening before my eyes.

Until one day in the middle of a shop I started freaking out. Crying and knowing that people were being killed – seeing and hearing them, and I knew I couldn't do anything to help. What good were my gifts if I was to be shown things happening in other countries that I was completely helpless to do anything about, and caused me to look like a crazy person losing it in public?

So for many years I went back to the old pattern of shutting it all down.

I made choices that I knew would numb me, lower my vibration and shut down my channel. I dated men who were abusive in different forms, I drank and partied and so many other things that will also need to go into another book! Let's not taint this one with my own personal history.

And then one day I met a man. (OK wait – so this time is different to the last story.)

I was invited to a talk in Sydney by a friend who told me she had a gut feeling I needed to come and hear the speaker that day. So I trusted her, went straight from the airport with my bags and rocked up to an old Pub in Sydney. I walked into the meeting room and chose a seat right up the front.

This tall lanky guy walked out dressed pretty casual for the event (I was of course in my designer business attire at the time,) and from the moment he opened his mouth I knew he was one of "my people"!

He spoke about Magick and how it had been part of his life since he was young and he talked about authors I had always wanted to read. He was there to talk about his fairly new modality and to be honest I had no idea what it was. At the time it made no sense to me at all but the feeling in my gut was that I had to find a way to afford it and commit right away. You know those sliding doors moments? This was one of those. I have no idea where my life would be if I didn't go along to the talk that day.

That modality was The Spiral and the "guy", who is now my dear friend and business partner, is Dane Tomas.

Going through The Spiral had started to shake things up for me and I was beginning to see and be conscious of the patterns in my life that had played out to get me to where I was. We had shone a light on them and released them, yet I knew there were big changes I needed to make in my life to reflect the changes I had made internally.

So as life does, it thew me a big wake-up call.

I was working way too hard working in corporate events, often working 7 days a week, sometimes up to 16 hours a day, living off energy drinks and sugar to keep myself going and living under very high stress and a lot of pressure.

One day I was running a big fancy dinner event for 350 people when I started getting pains in my chest, down my arms and tingling through my body. I felt nauseous, and I couldn't move from my chair. Oh shit – I knew something was seriously wrong.

But my work ethic was stronger than my own self-care.

I sat at that table sending a text message to my staff across the room to tell them what to do, and I plastered a well-practised fake smile on my face. Underneath that façade I was scared shitless. I knew this was serious and I might be in a lot of trouble but stubborn me was going to keep that fake smile on. I know people beside me on the table talked to me that night but I had no idea what they said, I just smiled and nodded politely hoping that was the right response. I didn't tell anyone what was happening. To this day, I don't know how I made it through that event and I get chills up my spine thinking about what could have happened.

The next day at the conference we happened to have a blood pressure testing stand there so I thought for some fun I would have a go. The man tested me once and said, "Something must be wrong," so he tested it again, and said, "Something must be wrong with that machine." He got out another machine, tested again and said, "I don't even know how you're sitting here with blood pressure this high! You need to get to a doctor immediately."

And even still, I didn't listen. (Stubborn much!! Cancerian with a Taurus Ascendant will do that to you.)

I packed down that event, organised couriers, got on a plane, and went home.

The next day I finally went to my family doctor and told her the story. She tested my blood pressure and again I received a confused and shocked response.

I was advised in a stern but caring tone that I was a very lucky woman to have not had a heart attack or a stroke, because that's what I was on the verge of. I was given strict instructions to take my own blood pressure 3 times a day, record it and send it to her.

She said, "I've never told anyone this before, but how quickly can you quit your job?!". I'm still grateful to her for that one question.

It was in that moment that I realised something. That I was putting everything and everyone else ahead of myself, and I would have allowed myself to die at that event in order to not let others down. I feel sick now looking back at that! What kind of person could be that lost in life that they would work themselves to death? I sure as shit didn't want to be that person.

Needless to say, that was a big wake-up call.

Within the month I closed my 2 businesses, packed up my house, put what I could in the car and drove myself to Byron Bay. I left behind my "designer life" with the wardrobe overflowing with designer outfits, shoes and handbags and went for a simple life.

I bought a caravan, put it on a property, and I lived in there for months, living a simple life, slowing right down, and realising that what I had been doing was numbing and avoiding myself for years. Trying to hide from the reality of who I really am and what my purpose is in life. Like maybe if I keep on constantly moving and being busy I won't have to admit that I have gifts that I am supposed to be using and honestly they scare the shit outta me. So rather than actually be myself, I will keep my head in a bucket of busy and pretend I can't see where I'm supposed to be.

From that day forward I promised myself, never again: that I would once again learn how to open my channel, learn how to trust my gifts, learn how to live in multiple dimensions without losing my shit in public, and so that's what I've been doing for the last 7 years.

I had recently become a practitioner of The Spiral (a modality that I have witnessed change countless lives for the better) and decided to dedicate myself to something that would help others not end up where I had been. Years later, and I am now a Co-Director of The Spiral Institute and lead Facilitator of the practitioner trainings, helping as many people as I can to let go of their conditioning and old stories, and to raise their vibration as I know that's what's needed for Humanity at this time.

Almost 3 years ago, with the support of Dane, I combined The Spiral with the Womb Gates and Womb Spiral was born. Now my biggest love is to work with women to clear and activate their Wombs, and with couples to consciously conceive babies. I have a group of women apprenticing with me and a number who are now qualified Womb Spiral practitioners.

For the last 2 years a lot of information about the Blue Diamond Souls has been downloading and it's finally time to share that with the world.

So now that I feel we have been introduced and you know a little backstory, here we are, ready to get into the juicy parts of the book.

MY FIRST MEETING WITH THE BLUE DIAMOND SOULS

The Blue Diamond Souls and the concept of Conscious Conception were unexpectedly introduced to me in a powerful setting in 2017. Ever since that moment I have been so captured by these Souls, how to support and honour them on their journey here to this dimension on Earth, and how to share the transmission of Conscious Conception to as many people as possible.

This is a deeply personal story of how they first appeared to me, and one I don't share publicly lightly. Yet, at the same time as it being incredibly private, I am committed to sharing all aspects of this journey knowing that opening myself up in service is also opening a Portal that is needed in the world.

So, deep breath and here we go.

First, let me tell you that for many years I tried to get pregnant... well that's what I told myself and my husband and following partner at the time. If I was to be completely honest with you here, when I was with my husband I would pray every day that I would not get pregnant knowing it was not a safe environment for a child to enter. I knew my own personal desire to be a mother was not worthy of causing another little being to be caught in the painful web of life I had chosen at the time.

All these years later I see the bigger picture – I am not here to birth one child – my Womb is here to support the birth of MANY!

This is the day I became a Soul Midwife.

In a sweet little hut in the countryside of New Zealand, my partner at the time and I were spending two quiet nights alone to rest and recover post a 6-week deep dive Immersion at Highden Mystery School before heading off for another Soul journey in Egypt. It was at a time in my life where I was starting the commitment of my life to a path of Soul initiation and finding my way to a heart-led life. Inviting my own Soul to finally come and rest at home in my heart.

My partner and I had spent the last 6 weeks practising Sacred Union – or love -making through the Womb Gates (see the section on Womb Gates for more info) and experiencing deep Shamanic journeys during our love-making sessions.

This particular day we had set up a potent Shamanic container and ritual as we headed into an afternoon of making love through the Gates. Taking ourselves into the Cosmic Womb, or the Void, the place of pure potentiality.

In that place, it's no longer an experience of you and me, and becomes one of union beyond the selves, a melting and dissolving into everything. In that moment as we reached the Cosmic Womb a storm started to brew outside, leading up to a sudden crack of thunder and lightning – and in that moment he ejaculated, which he would usually refrain from but the energy had taken us and we were no longer in a place of mind or control, something greater was moving us.

As we lay there in blissful silence I could feel the sensation and see the image of sperm meeting egg, vibrating together and eventually sperm entering the egg, feeling the egg start to divide... was this even possible? What could I be feeling? My partner looks at me with inquiry in his eyes... we had a moment of silent conversation, a knowing without words until one of us said... I think... did we... I think we just made a baby!

Both overwhelmed in tears of amazement, he went to catch some air outside.

As he was gone a Soul came through the window to talk with me.

Soul - Will you give everything for me?

Me - Yes of course?

Soul - Are you sure?

Me - Yes! Bring ALL of you – ALL of you is welcome here.

Whoa, did that just happen? The thoughts and feelings swirling through me in that moment felt like they must be palpable in the room.

When my partner came inside I went to tell him my experience but before I could he said, you won't believe it. A cloud was coming over the mountains, until I realised it was a Soul that came in through that window!

Well in that moment you could have picked me up off the floor.

Was this real? Was this even possible?

Well I mean, it must be, right? We both experienced it so it can't just be in my head.

Laying there in the magnitude of the moment, both in tears of gratitude, yet also the confusion of, can this be true? We start to giggle about how it arrived on a thunderclap! So clearly if we were pregnant we were going to have our hands full with our own little Thor.

A few days later, visiting the Pyramids, we head into the Great Pyramid and make our way up to the top chamber. Gratefully there was no one else there! Just a lovely security guard who seemed to really like us. With almost no English he gave us instructions that we could take turns laying down in the sarcophagus! WOW what an honour – so of course we jumped at it. As my partner was meditating inside the guard came to me, pointed to my tummy and said, "Baby?"

Whaaatttt – I was like – um, maybe? He pointed again, nodded his head and said, "Yes, 2 babies."

You could have knocked me over with a feather in that moment.

We left in silence.

We stood outside looking at each other with disbelief. Well maybe we are having Thor AND the Valkyries! We are going to need to call in all of our Shamanic mentors for this one!

Floating down the Nile a few days later with a powerful group of teachers and community we were anxiously waiting until it was time to do a pregnancy test and find out if we truly had conceived. Unfortunately we didn't need to wait long as my body showed me we were in fact not pregnant. After such an emotional few days that was a bitter pill to swallow and certainly a confusing time. For me personally, what I realised was that even though I was not pregnant with a child, I had received a powerful transmission on Conscious Conception that I was now able to share with others, and also that I still had communication with the Soul that came to me that day.

Since then I have met the Souls coming to other women's Wombs, but most importantly I have been able to communicate with the Collective of the Blue Diamond Souls so I can share with you what they have to say, who they are, why they are here and how we can best support them.

They have a powerful gift to share with us and they are here to make a rapid shift in Humanity.

WHO ARE THE BLUE DIAMOND SOULS

The next generation are the ones that are here to make rapid change in the world as we know it.

Creating a new Humanity.

These are the Blue Diamond Souls.

One of the biggest lessons they are here to teach us is to understand the vibration of Love, the 'I AM' presence, and to understand that not only is it possible, but it's imperative that we can make rapid change in the world.

Our purpose is to shift you as Humanity away from low density, third-dimensional beings heading towards rapid extinction, and instead to help you shift the vibration of this planet, of this Humanity, as we rise together, up to the fifth-dimensional realm that will allow you to see that life is in fact extremely different to the way that you have been viewing it.

And from this level, you will begin to see that we are all here to work together, not only on this planet, but also across other galaxies.

We are not individuals. We are all different aspects of the one organism who is here to activate the light codes and the light grids to shift all Humanity into a completely different dimension beyond what you are able to imagine.

Many of these Souls that are coming have not been here before, they've not been incarnated on this dimension of Earth before and they have a very different and very high vibration. If you've been around any of them, you would know something is very different about these children. You can see it in their eyes — they are AWAKE and alert. They are highly intelligent and they know things that may surprise you. They are not impacted by the same conditioning as us. Not born with the same ancestral conditioning you and I were. They're not willing to sit down and be quiet and to not be heard as they are here to make a shift and to make a change.

Change-makers don't sit quietly!

One example of these Souls is Greta Thunberg, a very young woman making waves in the world by being brave enough to stand up and speak! You will note she doesn't think she is brave, she doesn't see any other way. A Swedish environmental activist at 15, she is already making enough noise as one person speaking the truth, so can you imagine an entire generation of children like that, prepared to stand up and be themselves, born knowing their purpose! For big Corporations and Governments that's a threat — hence the push in vaccines, more poison in our food, water and air as it's best to keep us all numbed.

The Blue Diamond Souls are here to make monumental shift in the world. Then we start to realise that the reason that some people have considered not having children — because they worry about the state of the world — is perhaps the exact reason to have children. We need these Souls to incarnate here and to help us make the shift that's required.

These new Souls are asking to be born through activated Wombs and through conscious conception to parents who are letting go of their own conditioning and managing their own energy fields. It's a very different experience to parent these children and they will more than likely challenge your conditioned ways of being and of parenting.

Many of them are misunderstood, and many of them are being put on medications because people don't understand them. Think about the rise in ADHD or of children who we believe are on the Autism spectrum when actually many of them are just brilliant. Many of them are just very different, so we don't understand them, and some of these children are in fact Blue Diamond Souls.

Allowing them to explain in their own words where they are from:

Your planet and the way your people move upon this planet, you currently are living in what's called the 3D or third dimension, you are third-dimensional beings.

Yet your planet is currently also holding 12th-dimensional beings concurrently as is your earth moving at different frequencies. So, the land we come from, although appears invisible to you, is here within the same planet yet within a different dimensional field.

We come from the dimension where you call the Earth Lumeria. You think that this happened in a time gone by in the past, yet, as we've previously explained, as time is not linear, it is not happening necessarily in the past. Much of it is happening concurrently, yet in the dimensional realm that you are unable to see.

19

We are able to move through different dimensions. Although it becomes very uncomfortable for us, we are able to shift down to your third-dimensional reality. Mostly, we can make this shift when we are invited through a Portal, an opening in the time space continuum and in the dimensions for us to be able to travel between realms.

And so when these Portals are opened, it allows us to move from the 12th -dimensional plane into your third-dimensional plane and to be born into you as third-dimensional beings, humans.

Yet, where we are from our form is less physical, less dense, so we are able to move between time and space easily. So, although it seems confusing, we are already right here with you on this same planet.

OPENING THE PORTAL FOR THE BLUE DIAMOND SOULS

As I sit here, this is the most challenging part of the book for me to write because it's deeply personal and also because of the Sacredness of the moment, I want to be sure to hold the deepest of integrity to myself and the others present, and yet also share the story that is being asked of me to tell you. They (The Blue Diamond Souls) want you to understand how they are coming here and the importance of Temple or Ritual space in their conception and birth.

On my last visit to Highden Mystery School, the Portal opened to bring in tens of thousands of Blue Diamond Souls! I have experienced the Portal open before and bring up to 16 Souls through, but this time was overwhelmingly powerful and huge.

This is the story of that Portal opening. I invite you to keep an open mind as you read this and also you may wish to allow yourself to feel the transmission of this story as it is multi-dimensional.

One Friday morning I was with a small group up in the Turret doing our usual morning meditations together. Freezing cold and all rugged up in blankets, the only sound present was the birds waking up on the roof above.

Suddenly from the silence the message was so clear and strong. "Its time to open the Portal."

I instantly knew it was the voice of The Blue Diamond Souls and what I needed to do.

It was time to gather the community together and do a Ceremony to open the Portal calling in the Souls. The Souls of the Community, the Souls of the next generation and the connection to the World Soul.

I also knew that I needed to lay myself upon the Altar as a Womb that was inviting a Soul in. Knowing that my lack of attachment to the role of Mother was what was being asked for and that it was time to lay myself in full and Divine service to my Soul's purpose of supporting these BDS in finding their way to the Wombs and hearts of those who are destined to birth them.

The way these Souls are asking to be conceived is from a place of Sacredness and in an ultimate setting for the potential mother to be prepared to lay down her needs and desires of motherhood and instead lay herself upon the Altar in service of the possible Soul that may enter her Womb. To let go of any personal attachments to the outcome. I am not here to say that as a Collective we are at that stage yet but as this was the opening, that was to be my offering to the Temple. My own Womb.

> *We are calling to be conceived in Temple, in what we call Temple, in space of Sacredness, in a space of Love, in space of community. We are expecting to be honoured for who we truly are. We are expecting to be called in with reverence and Devotion. When I speak to the term Temple, remember that Temple can be created, with just two people coming into sacred union, or Temple can be created with an entire community coming into sacred union as one.*

In an ultimate world we would be called in by community and in an ultimate world will be called in by a group becoming one. Yet we understand that the human race is perhaps not yet in a place to understand such a vibration and frequency, though what we asked them to realise that it can also be done as two becoming one.

The Temple set, candles alight and the scents and sounds of Temple enticing us as we entered. My beloved and I lovingly guided to a bed up on the Altar, I feel my heart racing and the overwhelming expansion in my chest as I begin to settle into the magnitude of what is about to happen. Just as they have shown me many times over, we are going to bring forth The Temple that will open the Portal and guide these Souls through. I know this moment in time is one that can only ever truly be understood and shared by those who were there – and yet here we will be making a change in the future of Humanity.

To open this Portal is to journey to the Cosmic Womb, to the Void, the place of pure potentiality. This is the closest that you have to reaching our dimension. This is the closest meeting point between the realms. So for you to journey to the Cosmic Womb, and to call us, to simply welcome and call us in with Divine pure intention. The more of you that gather together at once to hold these Portals open, the more of us can come through to support you as Humanity.

And so, when done in community space, togetherness space, and each bringing yourselves to the Cosmic Womb together as one Collective, as one organism, not as a group of individuals, but as one organism, that vibration becomes strong enough to create a Portal that opens for long enough and magnetises many of us in.

Once a Portal has been opened that is large enough to bring through many, then as the individual couple it becomes easier to just tune in and tap into the fact that we are already in your dimension. So once again, to go to the Cosmic Womb yet understanding that we are already in your dimensional realm.

So allowing those whose purpose on this earth is to hold the Portal open for us, allowing and supporting those who understand the way to do this, so that then the individuals can more easily call us in to conceive.

Two High Priestesses gracefully used their voices, supported by the weaving of sounds that seemed to pick us up and take us on a journey to another realm, as another held her watchful gaze over the group, weaving the energy as required.

Together they guided the community through each of the Gates of the Womb. Dropping us in to trust and gratitude, leading into awe and devotion, coming back to the depth of Innocence that we are and diving in the deep, deep longing of the Womb.

As we begin to leave the Womb and head towards Creation point, we no longer seem to be in the same room. We have been transported to what feels like a Magickal Temple in another dimensional realm. I feel my body stand up and move towards the centre of the Altar. Standing with my back to the room I can feel the energy building, intensifying as we are coming closer to the final destination of the Cosmic Womb.

My beloved stands to join me with his chest pressed against my back and I feel held and safe, knowing what's about to come. The room moves into the Cosmic Womb, my hands shoot straight up in the air holding my Crystal Synergy Ankh pointing up to the sky and in that moment, it opens – the Portal to call in the Blue Diamond Souls. The surge of energy through my body and that of my beloved is immense, like being struck by a hit of lightning. I feel my knees struggling to hold me up and my beloved keeping us both balanced. It feels like we are there for lifetimes, surging and surging and then I see it. Here they come, I've seen them before as they enter the Portals but this time there's more.

I remember thinking, WOW there are hundreds of them.

Oh now wait – there are THOUSANDS AND THOUSANDS of them entering our dimension.

Slowly the energy of the room starts to make its way back down. Settling ever so gently back into this dimensional reality, back into the room, back into our bodies. Then it hits me. The magnitude of what this means. Tears flood down my face as I know this is my greatest purpose in this lifetime, to support these Souls in landing here, at this time when Humanity needs them the most.

Moments later a dear sister of mine in the space came over and said, "Did you see them? Thousands of stars came down." In that moment I knew it. I didn't just dream this. I'm not making up my own reality – this is really happening.

WHERE ARE THEY NOW?

Some of those Souls were conceived around the world that night, and many are here in our dimension waiting for the Wombs to be ready to hold them.

A few months later, a string of unlikely events lead me to meet a woman over dinner one night. As we chatted about life and Wombs and Blue Diamond Souls (as often comes up in conversation with me) she asked to share something with me. Saying, "I don't know why I feel I need to tell you this, but I'm pregnant and I haven't really told anyone yet."

Well, you guessed it – we worked out the dates and it was on that very night that she conceived.

These Souls led us together to meet that day and for her to share that with me so I could continue to get the proof my poor mind seems to need that all of this is really happening.

I also know of another woman who conceived that very night too.

As for the rest, perhaps that's why you're reading this book? Is one of them coming through you or your loved ones? Or perhaps it's time to start preparing for one?

ACTIVATING THE WOMB

MY JOURNEY WITH THE WOMB

My story of my own Womb is very much like many women's, one of disconnection and trauma, and quite frankly an inconvenience.

It was the part of my body that had let me down, held pain and past trauma that I didn't want to face, and to be totally honest, if you had told me years ago that I should activate my Womb or do "Womb work", I would have thought you were a little crazy and probably wanted to get away from you as fast as possible. I think on some unconscious level I knew that to look there would be like opening Pandora's box, forcing me to look at things I would rather pretend never happened.

I thought bleeding monthly was an inconvenience, and quite frankly wished it would not happen. I did my best to ignore it and surge on with my day like nothing was different. I mean what good could come from allowing myself to actually "feel" what was happening in my body? Best try to ignore it, right? Um… NO!!

At the very young age of 16 I had managed to get myself into a situation I was not mature enough to handle – and to be honest neither were my friends who were thrown in the position of having to support me.

I had been the girl with massive "stop abortion" signs on my bedroom walls! And here I was in a situation where I knew the best decision was to actually do the one thing I judged most in the world. One day I tore down those signs and resigned myself to the fact that I was not in a situation where I could have this baby that was growing inside me. Tearing down those signs felt like tearing a hole in my heart and the devastation of that experience shut me down completely!

Walking up to the clinic doors I was faced with women with the same signs I previously had on my wall, yelling at me that I was going to go to hell and I was a murderer! The only way I knew how to deal with the shame was to disappear so far inside myself and vow to never ever come out again. Choosing to numb myself to life was all I could manage in that situation and at the time it seemed to protect me from the cavernous hole of sadness and shame I was being sucked in to. I learnt that day that life provides us with the ultimate mirror for our own growth and the things we judge will come back to haunt us. I found compassion for others when I realised sometimes the actions we take, that we think are with care for others, are actually deeply traumatising to another when you don't know their circumstances.

In my 20s I experienced the crippling pain of Ovarian cysts and at the time I couldn't afford to get them treated. To be honest, I took this on as my punishment for the actions of my 16-year-old self. During sex my Cervix would often be extremely painful, so I used that as another doorway into my own shutting down and numbness, I didn't dare admit I was in pain to my partner and would take solace in the fact my face could hold a poker face and not let him know I was in excruciating pain. I just figured my body was there for his pleasure and not mine. Now when I look back at this I have tears that stream down my face, as I see how I allowed myself to be further traumatised completely unnecessarily. I thought my body wasn't my own – I mean I didn't really like it much anyway, so why not just let someone else get pleasure from it?

The rest of the time I was completely numb. My Womb was numb, my body was numb! I now understand that my body was in fact in 'freeze'! No wonder life just didn't seem to have much feeling to it, people would say I felt cold to them. Um, yeah that's because I didn't feel anything so I couldn't understand how to be overly warm and loving toward people. I now understand it was all linked! My Womb and my Sex being in freeze made it feel numb and basically that lead to an inability to really connect deeply with anyone.

In my late 20s and my 30s I tried to conceive and I couldn't. I decided that quite clearly my body was again just punishing me for what I had done at 16 and I shut down even more! Clearly my body was completely useless! At least that's the story I started to buy into.

If you had told me back then that I was going to end up working with women all over the world to help them heal their Wombs, connect more deeply to their own bodies and have amazing sex and love lives of depth with their partners, I would have thought you were crazy. If you had told me I would be using that work to help couples conceive high vibration Souls, I would have literally walked away shaking my head.

Yet in 2015 that all changed!

One day working inside a big shipping container converted to an office with a lot of other people, I had a life-changing premonition. Working on a massive outdoor event – hot, noisy, crammed into a big metal sardine tin – I heard a voice, it simply said, "Kundalini Dance". I looked around thinking it was someone else, until I realised it was a message of some sort. I had never heard of Kundalini and I hadn't danced since I was a teenager but I decided to type it into Google and see what happened. I literally almost fell off my chair when I saw a course to become a Kundalini Dance Facilitator.

A few months later I was on a plane to Bali to spend a month training as a Kundalini Dance Facilitator. "Corporate chick" on a plane to go hang out with "Hippies" hahahaha. Literally I couldn't have made more of a flip in direction in my life. Yet as you know from my earlier story, I had gone through The Spiral and life was changing rapidly! I can guarantee that 'pre-Spiral me' would NOT have gotten on that plane to Bali, but here I was knowing I could make my own choices in life – finally!

So here I was in Bali wearing "goddess clothes" and clearing stagnant emotions and energies of myself and others through dance. I finally started to feel my body more and more and start to make it my home. I opened up to connecting to my own sexual energy, which was completely new for me. I mean I literally had no idea that was a thing! Then I began to understand that it's not only important in my life, it actually IS my life-force! I mean, why had no one ever told me that my sexual energy and my life-force energy were not only connected but were basically one and the same! No wonder I felt kinda dead and numb in life. The changes my body went through that month were life-changing. I could not only feel myself, I could feel others and that was literally revolutionary for me. I could not only now begin to connect more deeply to myself but for the first time in my life, I was able to connect deeply with other women.

I could now not only feel and move my own energy but I could also move and transmute the energy of a room. That completely fascinated me and, to this day, is a gift I am deeply grateful for.

My Kundalini activated and I started to feel my body as a fully alive being! Suddenly an entirely new world opened up and I realised I could experience orgasmic pleasure through my entire body just from the feeling of the sun or the wind on my skin. My old self would have thought I was crackers if I knew that was possible! Now I know it's not only possible, it's my birthright to feel so alive. It's also a gift the womb-en who apprentice with me are benefitting from!

I truly felt like I had just woken up from some kind of strange slumber. How did it take me this long to start to live?

It's also where the name Zapheria was born. It's where I owned what had already opened up in me from doing The Spiral, the part of me that I had kept hidden most of my life.

A week later I was attending an ISTA (International School of Temple Arts) Spiritual, Sexual and Shamanic Experience in Byron Bay. Whoosh, now that was an eye opener and a completely new experience that again changed the trajectory of my path. In honouring of the Sacredness of the work I don't feel to share the details, but we were doing a ritual that activated the Womb. I didn't even know that was a thing! Yet that experience opened me up to begin to see the door to the Mysteries; to understand that the Womb is more than a baby-making machine and a place of painful bleeds. It's the most potent feminine Portal to the Mysteries. It's the seat of our Feminine Intuition. It's the key to more than I ever imagined possible.

That evening laying in bed I was beyond amazed that my Womb was literally pulsating! It felt like something was alive in there... A little disconcerting at first and I wondered if I was maybe going a little crazy and imagining things, until my lover at the time said he could feel it too!

31

That day I knew the Womb was part of my purpose and this was a path I would follow from then on. If I could go from feeling numb to life and shut down, to feeling so alive I was bursting out of my skin, then I wanted to help other women experience the same awakening.

I decided then and there I would do all I could to journey much deeper with the woman who ran that ritual, and so that's what I did. For the next 2 years I attended Janine MaRae's retreats and as many ISTAs that she was facilitating as I could. Gratefully I was later accepted into her 12-month apprenticeship and I haven't looked back since.

Following that, as you know, Womb Spiral was born and now the Womb Spiral Apprenticeship Program. What a deep, deep honour it is to be now apprenticing so many amazing women into the work I've been creating. The Womb and the Blue Diamond Souls are my love and my life, my way of assisting the rise in consciousness of Humanity and the planet.

So here I am, a woman who went from being a scared and shut-down shell of a person, to a fully alive, open and loving woman following the divine calling of the Soul. I know you can do that too, and in fact, that's what I want for you.

HOW CAN YOU START TO CONNECT TO YOUR WOMB?

As a human race we are disconnected from The Womb!

Our own, The Collective, Mother Earth's and the Cosmic Womb.

Women used to go to the Red Tent to bleed together. We would spend that time in Sacredness together. Sharing stories, doing ceremonies, creating Magick and connecting to the cycles of the Earth. When the women came home they would report to the village all predictions for the next cycle of the moon; when it was time to seed, when to harvest, when the weather would change. Women were so connected to The Womb that they could feel "Her" – The Earth, Mother Nature, The Moon, The Goddess – and were they Divinely connected.

The Feminine has been rising for years, and now the Womb of the world is rumbling, waking up as more and more of us are Activating our Wombs and starting to work with Her again.

They say when women awaken, mountains move.

I feel that when Wombs awaken the ripple is felt across the entire planet and beyond.

What's important to speak to here is that you do not have to have a physical Womb to be able to work with The Womb, or even to activate your Womb. Everybody has an Etheric Womb and each and every one of us can be connected to the Collective Womb, which means every one of us can make an impact

> So let's take a moment to start connecting you to your Womb.
>
> Read this and then give it a try.
>
> You can also find a meditation in the bonus material at the back of the book.
>
> Place your hands on your lower tummy below the belly button. To give you a visual, the Womb is about the size of an Avocado and is about 3 finger width below the belly button.

Close your eyes and spend a few moments simply focused on the breath. Allow yourself to come to centre.

Bring your attention down to your Womb space under your hands and imagine you can send your breath right into the Womb.

Stay with this for a few minutes and just observe.

Do you feel anything? Is there lack of any feeling? Not making anything right or wrong, just observing.

This is a great start – just to allow your focus to start observing what's present – even if what's present is nothing. You may want to try this a few times and see what changes.

If you want to go a little further you could spend more time here and imagine you can drop your consciousness down into your Womb space. Don't worry yourself with the head side of things – no trying to get it right or second guess yourself – just do it and see what happens.

Again spend some time here and observe what you feel, or don't feel. Try it for a few days and witness what changes.

When you feel ready to take the practice further you may like to visualise an umbilical cord that, whilst it remains connected to your Womb, drops down into the Earth. Seeing, feeling or imagining this cord dropping down through all the layers of the Earth. The crust, down into the mantle, the outer core and eventually finding its way to the inner core, the centre of the Earth, her Womb.

Feel your body as that connection is made and notice how centred and stable you become.

You may wish to breathe her love and her life-force up through your grounding cord and into your own Womb. Creating the connection from your Womb to Earth Womb.

The Womb is powerful at transmuting that which no longer serves us, so this connection can also help to release old and stagnant energy from the Womb and give it down to the Earth Womb as she can send it back as love and life-force.

See, feel or visualise your "umbilical grounding cord" come back up out of the

Earth to your own body.

You may then want to go into nature and rest for a moment with your feet on the ground, to ground your energy back into the present moment.

If you bleed, some other ways you may like to start connecting to your own Womb is to track your cycle, "consciously bleed" and perhaps even work with the blood.

If you don't already track your cycle, tracking is a great way to start to connect more with your Womb and, of course, your own cycles. I personally use an app called "Clue" as I love the simplicity of it, the graphics and the fact I can share my cycle with my partner if I choose to. There are plenty of similar apps out there so find one that works for you, or do the "old-fashioned" way and note it down in coloured pens on your calendar.

If you really want to connect more deeply to your cycles, your Womb and your blood, I would recommend trying a Mooncup. This way you can get a really good idea of what your flow is like, the colour and consistency, and it allows you to create a relationship with your blood. You may even choose to start placing it in the Earth each month to connect into the cycles of the Earth and nature more, or even doing ritual with it. You can buy Mooncups at your local health food store or there are many options online. They are a small "cup" that you place inside to capture the blood. This may seem a little unusual at first but after one or two cycles you will get the hang of it. I remember the first time someone suggested this, I thought it was a terrible idea but as soon as I tried it, I experienced the profound shift of finally connecting more deeply to my own body.

*I am a big believer in ritual with menstrual blood, however keep in mind it is the most powerful Magick you can do, so if you don't know what you're doing I would leave it or find someone to teach you. We cover it in one of my courses which can be found on my website.

The Womb is always either holding (to keep a baby in) or releasing and shedding. Even if you're past menopause, when you stop bleeding you still energetically go through the cycles. So you can choose to consciously release each month. Rather than ignore the bleed or go on as usual, you can spend some time journalling or meditating on what you are letting go of from this last month. What emotions, stories, and experiences are you letting go of? Either just making the intention this bleed dedicated to letting go, or doing your own ritual around it, perhaps writing it on a piece of paper and burning it.

WHAT IF YOU DON'T HAVE A PHYSICAL WOMB?

For women who don't bleed, you still bleed and cycle energetically. In fact, the Crone or Wise Woman is at her most powerful as she can connect to her cycle at anytime of the month. She is also often at her juciest so don't believe the stories that have been so deeply conditioned they become truth for many, that non-bleeding women dry up... it can be quite the opposite! I will share resources in the back.

Women who have had the Womb removed – you still have an Etheric (Energetic) Womb and it is just as powerful as any woman with a physical Womb. Perhaps you have heard of the phenomenon of people having limbs removed and still feeling them? The physical can be removed and still leave behind the etheric/energetic. It's no different for the Womb. The physical can be removed, yet the energetic, etheric remains.

For anyone not born with a Womb you do have an Etheric Womb so you can still connect to it, activate it and choose to energetically bleed if you so choose.

Even though you may not be as interested in the Womb Activation for yourself, you can choose to hold the activation for the Collective Womb. More on this on page 67.

RELEASING TRAUMA FROM THE WOMB

As I mentioned before, the Womb either holds (a baby) or they release and shed. Her power is to be able to shed wounds and traumas and transmute them, however most people don't know this and so instead their Womb is still holding all of their past traumas.

This includes:

- Sexual trauma from abuse, either from others or even from ourselves, where sex has been engaged in either non-consensually or before the body was actually ready.

- Birth trauma from complications during pregnancy and/or the birth process.

  Also the loss of any pregnancies either as miscarriage, stillborn or abortion.

- Conditioned trauma placed on us by others, either by their religious views/ beliefs or family constructs that have created fear and shame about your body or your sexuality. For example, being told it's a sin to feel sexual, have sex, engage with the same sex, touch your own body, and so the list goes on. Or religious views that still believe in and practise mutilation of a woman's genitals.

- Physical trauma from conditions such as endometriosis, ovarian cysts, hysterectomies or any other manner of physical ailments to the Womb and the Sex organs.

- Past lives can also impact the emotional blockages or traumas we hold within the Womb, and if you consider that time is in fact not linear you may realise these lifetimes are likely to be running concurrently and can greatly impact your current perspectives.

WHAT ABOUT LINEAGE/ANCESTRAL WOUNDS?

Do you realise you were physically inside your grandmother's Womb? I remember the first time I heard this I was blown away.

When women are born, they already have all the eggs the ovaries will produce in their lifetime.

So you actually started out as an egg inside your mother's Womb when she was inside her mother's (your grandmother's) Womb. Trippy right?!

So if you look back to what was happening in your grandmother's life at the time your mum was born, you may be able to find a connection to some, or even many of your unconscious patterns and even your Womb story.

You can look at the trauma you may be holding in your Womb, or in your body, the learnt conditioning and the stories/beliefs you run and see that some – if not many – may not actually be yours. Even if they did not start with you, you have the power to release and heal them for your lineage 7 generations forwards and 7 generations backwards.

It's a powerful exercise to look back to how your grandmother's life was – what challenges was she facing? War, famine, poverty, etc.? Then look to your own patterns that play out in your life – for example, having money stories that you cant seem to shift, and then looking back to the fact that your grandmother lived in poverty. Or having issues around overeating, and realising your grandmother lived in famine.

You have the ability to break through these old stories when you can see where they came from.

> Take some time to write out your grandmothers life experience
> You may need to ask other family members what her life was like Consider things like her financial status,

her love life, how many children she birthed and what the births were like, what was happening culturaly for her and anything that would impact her base survival needs like famine, war or diseases

Next start to compare each area of your life to hers
Eg
Financial
Health
Cultural Issues
Religeous beliefs
Love life
Birthing children

Where do you find either similarities, or polarities
Chose what areas you would like to work on and spend some time consciously untangling your beliefs to those that have been unconsciously insilled in you.

WHAT IS AN ACTIVATED WOMB & WHY WOULD YOU WANT ONE?

There is the physical Womb (if you were born with one) and then there's the Etheric Womb, which all beings have. The Etheric or Energetic Womb is the one we can "activate". Yet for most people it will remain fairly dormant until you choose to work with it.

You are an energetic being, so you can choose to activate a certain frequency within your own field. An Activated Womb is simply activating the energetic field of the Womb. It's like waking it up from its long slumber and realising that it is in fact your birthright to have an Activated Womb.

Often people ask, "What does it feel like?". Well for me when it first activated it was intense! Like something was coming

40

alive inside my tummy. A really strong current like electricity pulsing through it. For many though, it's more like a tingling feeling that starts up in the Womb, or little flutters and pulses.

Energy is a frequency, so you can simply choose to learn to use that frequency. Just like a radio station is tuned in to a certain frequency, you can do the same with your own energy fields and so the same with an Activated Womb.

Because it's a frequency and we are energetic beings, one Activated Womb can also activate another. Therefore we can all support the activation and raise the vibration of the Collective Womb for the arrival of the Blue Diamond Souls for ourselves and for others.

Once you activate the Womb you can begin to feel that within the Earth Womb there is an Ecstatic current that can literally lead you where to go next in your life. When you activate your Womb and connect into the Ecstatic current of the Earth, you can choose to surrender to the flow of life in a new way. Letting go of the need to control the outcomes all the time and learning that there is always a greater intelligence at play, if you choose to connect to it.

In 2016 when I was deepening into how to live a Womb-guided life and committed to embodying the feminine flow at an entirely new level, I went alone to Vietnam for a month. I went with the one intention of learning to follow the Ecstatic current at all times in my life. I knew spending a full month following the Ecstatic Current was going to be a challenge, but I also knew it would initiate me into a new level of Womb connection. I had tried similar things for a day at a time, or whilst walking out in nature, but by heading to a totally new environment and doing it for so long, I knew it was going to be a huge step in my own evolution.

41

Day 1 I can honestly say I couldn't get a grasp on it at all! I was in a big city in a completely new energy, away from the land that my body already knew the vibration of, and it was confusing. A few days in and things started to settle. I could feel my own Womb communicating with the land there and a gentle pull guiding me on where to go next.

From then on that's all I did, follow the current, and if I couldn't feel it I would just sit down and wait. I didn't have any accommodation booked, no plans – nothing. Just feel and listen.

My rule was I don't move unless I feel pulled, drawn to move and I don't use my head to make any decisions along the way. For a FULL month! WOW some amazing things happened that trip but this one stands out.

I woke up one day and as per usual just started to follow the "pull" Walking along a street I came across a very rough and steep driveway that climbed up the side of a big hill. The "pull" was to walk up there! I stood at the bottom for a moment thinking what on earth am I doing - and then I started to walk up it.

Half way up I came across an older lady resting part way up. She smiled at me so I assumed I must be ok and kept walking up. As I got to the top of the hill there was a massive Gold Buddha towering above me......whaaaatttt - this was not at all visible from the street and I had clearly taken a back entrance to this place that I soon discovered was a Monastery.

I looked around a little and ended up seeing the lady again. She waved me over to sit on the chair beside her and as I did she took my hand and gently smiled at me. She spoke no English and me no Vietnamese so it was a beautiful communication without words.

She signalled for me to wait where I was and she went to speak to someone, then coming back she waved me to join her. No idea what was happening I trusted and went with her to a room where they dressed me in robes. Next I was ushered to a bigger room with a large central Altar. I slowly discovered I had been invited to join the private class for the entire day! Welcomed in with open arms by the Women I joined in the teachings and was accepted as one of them. No idea what the Priest said I had to rely only on feeling the transmission of the teachings. It was profound!!! Often with tears rolling down my face I prayed and meditated with them all day.

At one point the Priest called me over and with his limited English he told me I was being welcomed home and that he was giving me my Buddhist Dharma name! I don't feel to share it but its meaning is very large predestined affinity. By the reaction of the other Women I knew this was a honour!

That's just one example of the Magick on that trip.

Since then I've learnt not to question my Womb or the Ecstatic current again.

> Try it for yourself sometime
>
> Go out into nature to an area you feel comfortable and make sure you don't have a time limit to stick to. Take water and food and anything else you may want with you and turn off your phone so there are no distractions.

Sit on the earth and close your eyes

Spend some time just breathing and bringing your attention inwards to your own body.

Do the Womb connection exercise on page 33

When you feel centred within yourself then start to bring your attention to your surroundings

See if you can feel the Earth, the plants, the air on your skin

Now can you feel an energy that's inviting you to move your body in any certain direction? Just follow it for a while. No need to understand it.

Maybe you will sit in the one spot and not feel anything

Maybe you will be called to stare at a flower or a tree for a while and then something will capture your energy to move.

Just play with it for a while

If you feel an energy that seems to move you – that's the Ecstatic Current

If you don't – try again sometime

The Womb is the seat of the Feminine, so when she is activated most people find they are more connected to their inner Feminine, no matter what gender, if any, they identify as. Connecting more deeply to their own authentic feminine power, which it turn connects you more to your intuition. If you connect to Her she will talk to you, give you answers and guidance in your life. Connecting to the Womb, connecting to your own Feminine more deeply also connects you to your our own body, sensuality and sexuality. Becoming more orgasmic and finding deeper connection with yourself and with others. Even opening up an entirely new level of possibility in love-making, or Sacred Union.

Some of the things I hear women say after journeying Womb Spiral or Womb Activations with me are that they:

- Are connected to their own bodies
- Find connection to their Soul's path
- Experience more pleasure in daily life
- Feel more nurturing and loving towards themselves and others
- Feel more connected to their partners and their families
- Feel more connected to pleasure, sensuality and sexuality
- Have an improved sex life with their partners
- Feel connected to their own intuition
- Create deeper connections with other women
- Earn more money
- Manifest and create easily
- Conceive with more ease and more likely to experience easeful birth
- Attract more opportunities and people into their lives
- Free themselves from past trauma and lineage wounds
- And so the list goes on…

The Womb is the place of creation, so as you connect more deeply to your own Womb it becomes natural to follow the cycle of creation in your own life; to step into the realisation that you can be your own Master Creator: conceiving, gestating and birthing your own ideas, projects, creations and even yourself over and over. So it's important to realise the Womb is for creating more than human life. It's for birthing all you desire in this lifetime.

You may choose to activate your Womb for many reasons.

You may want to activate your Womb for the same purposes as I write this book – to bring in the next generation and to create an environment that is welcoming to the Blue Diamond Souls.

Raising the vibration of your own Womb is at the forefront of what you can do to ensure your body is able to hold one of these children, as – through almost no fault of your own – it's quite possible if you have not done any Womb work, that the vibration of your Womb may be very dense. It's subject to the life we lead, being around so many different technologies, laptops and wifi. The food we eat, the water we consume, the air we breathe and of course the emotions we carry are all contributing factors.

The body of a woman holds a physical womb, the body of all beings holds an energetic womb. So you are made up of a physical body and you are also equally made up of an energetic body, it is equally as important as your physical body, in actual fact, for us, it is even more of a high priority than what your physical body is.

And so to look at the aspects of the physical Womb, the physical job of conceiving and of holding and of growing the child, yet the energetic Womb of the woman is what actually starts to hold us with our energetic imprint for being born. As we have said many times before, on how sensitive we are to energy to vibration to frequency, we desire to be held within a space that is an energetic container that is energetically activated, that is energetically alive and working with us as when we are in the womb. We are also, as well as creating our physical body, we are also creating our energetic body and so, we require both a physical womb and the energetic womb to both be involved in the gestation of us as we lead towards birth. An Activated Womb is simply the energetic aspect of the Womb that is also awake, it is alive. It is a vibrating, pulsating, alive being in and of itself. It works in conjunction with the physical Womb, so many women can conceive and birth through only the physical Womb alone. Yet the impact that that has on the energetic body of the child is great as they are being held in a denser and lower vibration. And we are asking to be born into a higher vibrational field that is supportive of who we are. We also request that the Womb be in what we call an activated state in the woman because it brings her into deeper connection with herself and her own body, she becomes more aware of her inward being, of being able to be fully present in the moment in her body and therefore is able to connect more deeply to us. She is able to feel the nuances, she is able to feel that we are in her Womb, she is able to feel and connect to us at all times. Also, it makes it easier for her to communicate with us. As when we are in the Womb, we are constantly energeticall communicating with the woman, with the mother. And from this space, when she has it activated, she is more likely to be able to hear and understand us and communicate with us right from the moment of conception all the way through till birth. So, in fact, an Activated Womb makes a drastic difference for us in the conception process, in the gestation process and also in the birthing, as an Activated Womb is more likely to be able to remain completely connected to us through the birthing process. She is more alive and moving and working together as one in the birthing process. And this to us is extremely important. And so for these reasons, we are coming through women with an Activated Womb and this is of high importance, a high priority to us.

My presentation at the Seven Sisters Women's Festival in VIC, Australia in 2017 is a beautiful example of how just Activating the Womb can be enough for some women who have struggled to conceive, or carry full-term, can shift their Womb vibration enough to being able to birth a beautiful healthy child. During that session we did a powerful Womb Activation journey together. To this day the memory of that moment is still so powerful for me, and many women still speak of it to me.

Fifteen minutes before I was to go on stage that day I went backstage to do some clearing and to drop in to my own Womb. There was a small handful of women sitting in the tent ready for the session to commence, and not many other women in sight at the time. I dropped into my Womb and asked her to call in the women who would benefit the most from my session and as I did I saw big wings come out of my womb and start to call women in to the tent. I stayed with that for about 5 minutes and when I walked back out into the tent it was FULL and more women were flooding in. Women feel the call of the Womb even if they are not consciously aware of it.

Close to 500 women in a tent that day and almost everyone in that session had a Womb activation. There were women howling, women crying, women laughing, women in yelps of celebration and the energy was literally palpable. All I did that day was get out of the way and allow the Womb to do her magick. I surrendered to a greater calling and I allowed the transmission to move through me and into the women.

For an hour after that session I stood there as women lined up to say thank you or ask questions. One woman told me that she had been pregnant 6 or 7 times but never been able to carry to full term. As she shared her story I could feel the depth of pain she felt about that, yet at the same time I could feel the shift that had occurred for her in that session. I lost contact with her after that day and often wondered how she was. Until 2019, at the same festival, when her mother came to find me to say her daughter was soon to have a baby!!! Both her mother and I were in tears as she thanked me for that session, and I know that is a moment I will remember forever.

That's what I do this work for, those moments of knowing a new Soul has found a safe Womb and a beautiful couple have had their dreams come true. That same festival, 2 other women came and told me similar stories of conceiving shortly after that session. Who knows how many more there are that I don't know about, but one thing I know for certain is that Womb work is potent and much needed at this time on Earth.

WHAT ARE THE WOMB GATES?

The Womb Gates are a natural journey of progression that opens the flow of feminine or Shakti energy all the way from the woman's Sacred entrance, the first step of entering a woman's Temple, the Yoni (Sanskrit word for Vagina) lips and all the way to connect to the Cosmic Womb; the place of pure potentiality where all of creation is from, and where Souls enter this realm. An energetic pathway from the Yoni lips to the Cosmic Womb, the Womb Gates are teachings from a long lineage of Feminine Mystery holders. Those who dedicate themselves to the deep journeying of the Gates can find along its path a treasure trove of access points to awaken the deepest of the mysteries of the feminine. Opening to the truth that you have access to become your own Master Manifester by connecting to the Quantum field of pure potentiality that awaits you in the Cosmic Womb. You begin to realise your birthright is to be fully connected to all that is, through the Temple of your own body.

My intention here is to provide you with a glimpse into the Womb Gates as these could be a full book, and a lifetime of journeying in themselves, and to truly know the Womb Gates is to experience and embody the teachings rather than to read about them. As with any great teachings there are layers upon layers that open up as you deepen your practices with them; the Womb Gates open up mysteries within mysteries as they guide you deeper and deeper into their gifts. After 5 years of dedicated practice with the Gates I still consider myself a student to them and they are forever showing me new ways to work with them. Deeper and deeper into the Temple mysteries they take me and the more my body comes to life with all that they offer.

The Womb Gates are the foundation for Womb Spiral and working with the Womb Gates is the single most powerful way I have found for working with the Womb and especially for clearing emotional blockages, traumas and wounds that we carry from the past.

The Gates are a powerful way to call in and consciously conceive a child and also to open up to the possibility of Ecstatic birthing.

On a very surface level I have also worked with the Gates in friendships and relationships, following the natural progression to consciously deepen the connection. One particular relationship that comes to mind was with a beautiful man a few years ago. We weren't really sure if we were just great friends or if something else was going to grow from that friendship. Starting the relationship slowly, finding our way naturally until one day it was clear there was a trust that had formed between us. Both recognising that, our hearts opened even more to each other as the first gate between us opened. Soon after, laying together sharing our hearts, each of us burst into tears of deep, deep gratitude of one another. A few weeks later my devotion to him opened so deeply all I could imagine was being there in deep support of his journey, beyond any personal feelings I may be holding, my devotion to him was that his heart may find true love. I was able to see in his eyes the Divine innocence of a pure heart.

Some teachings may tell you the only way to truly open the Womb Gates is with a beloved in Sacred Union. To some extent I understand why they share this teaching as to make love through the Womb Gates with a partner who is at the same level of evolution is an incredibly potent experience and it was a critical part of my own path. However, I feel this teaching is very limited and not completely true. Some of my most profound journeys through the Womb Gates were with my teacher, who – with Shamanic practices – guided a room full of people, in their own space and fully clothed through the Gates. Perhaps for many in the room it was merely a taster and not something they could then attain on their own, but it is still a deeply potent transmission of the work. For anyone wanting to journey the Gates alone, like any spiritual practice you can choose to journey it alone and in Divine communion with God consciousness in the place of a partner.

You may find slightly different versions of the location of the 7 (or 8) Gates depending on the translation. I choose to follow those my teacher shared with me as when I feel the flow in my body these make the most sense.

In my current offerings I take clients through the Womb Gates in Womb Spiral and my Apprentices spend an entire month with each Gate before their initiation where we journey the Gates as 7 Initiation rituals.

FIRST GATE - TRUST AND THE YONI LIPS (VAGINA LIPS)

Clearing: This first gate is where Trust may be broken, either by another or by oneself with unwanted touch or penetration before the body is truly open and ready. To clear this Gate is to release the emotional history where Trust has been lost.

Conception: Trust in yourself, Trust in your partner, Trust in the Soul you are calling in and Trust in the greater picture; conception will happen in the perfect moment for the higher order of things. To consciously conceive is to move through Trust within yourself and with your partner.

Birthing: For birth the Gates are opened in reverse and so at the final Gate the baby is able to receive the imprint and vibration of Trust from the mother. Giving the child the gift of beginning this life feeling Trust is a monumental offering. For many of us we have arrived here through a birth that may not have been as nurturing as we may have liked, especially considering what generation you are in, it's quite possible you were born in a time where it was normal to take the baby from the mother before there is any bonding touch. Either to clean and swaddle the baby before they are given to mum, or maybe also taken to another room altogether, in the name of giving mum some rest time. It's very difficult to Trust the world if your introduction to it is strangers' hands, bright lights and being removed from your mother.

Life: By moving beyond the places you have built up an inability to Trust, you can begin to connect to what Trust truly means. As an example, if situations happened in your life that perhaps made you not trust a certain sex, or a certain type of person, you are now disconnected from your true compass of trust. Deciding, for example, all men are not to be Trusted, may lead you to believe you can Trust women over men... it may seem fair to you at the time but what if there is a situation where you need to Trust one of 2 people and one of them is a man? You will follow your broken compass and Trust the woman before you even feel which one you truly can Trust.

Exercise: Take some time to journal about Trust.

Who/what do you Trust? Why? Is this actually true or is it through an old filter you're running? Who/what don't you Trust? Why? Is this actually true or is it through an old filter you're running?

If you are more of an embodied person you may choose to dance Trust. Put on some music, close your eyes and drop into your body. Now allow Trust to move you, to guide you and show you, tell you a story.

Also see the free Trust journalling exercise in the free bonus resources.

SECOND GATE - GRATITUDE AND THE G-SPOT

Clearing: To be able to hold the true vibrational frequency of Gratitude is a profound feeling. One that wells up with often unexpected emotion. Stepping beyond simply speaking the word as a shallow term, and rather fully feeling it. When you can clear the G-Spot and the second Gate, you open to the beautiful upwelling of Gratitude. Holding this level of Gratitude opens a new experience of life. How would life be different if the Gratitude of simply seeing the sunrise moved you, or the touch of your partner filled your body with so much Gratitude it allowed your heart to swell with Love?

Conception: Gratitude for your body, for your experience of pleasure, for all that your partner brings to your life, for your love for one another. Riding the wave of Gratitude opens up a deeper level of love-making and a higher vibrational field to call in the Soul. To look into your partner's eyes as they well with tears of Gratitude for the love you both hold in that moment is a profound heart-opening experience.

Birthing: Giving your child the gift of feeling your Gratitude for their birth, for their life, for all that they are, welcomes them to an environment where they know they are welcome, wanted and that it is safe to bring all of themselves. No need to do or be anything other than their Divine Soul in all of its expression in the world.

Life: The G-Spot is also the fountain of the Sacred Waters. For some women the connection to their G-Spot allows the Amrita to flow naturally. Water is in fact the portal to the feminine intuition and the G-Spot is one gateway to connect to the natural flow of the Feminine and intuition.

Exercise: Journal prompt - what are you truly grateful for?

Also see the Gratitude meditation exercise in the free bonus resources.

THIRD GATE - DEVOTION AND THE CLITORIS

Clearing: For many the Clitoris has been approached with anything other than Devotion, yet it is the part of a woman's body that is quite literally there for her pleasure, holding more than 8,000 nerve endings in the tip alone. If you truly consider this – I don't know about you but to me it certainly brings a sense of awe that the body has created such a powerful centre in a woman's body. Releasing the times the Clitoris has been treated with anything other than Devotion can allow a woman to drop into the depth of honouring the body, especially considering the Yoni is her Temple and the Clitoris is right there at the head of the Temple door.

Conception: During a love-making ritual to bring in the energy of Devotion, seeing one another as the Divine allows you to move past the personal, and step into the magnitude of the realisation that we are all in fact Divine and worthy of Devotion. To bring a child into the world with the Sacredness of Devotion is a key aspect in conceiving a Blue Diamond Soul.

For the couple who are merging in Sacred union, they are coming to this place of Temple together, where they are able to see each other as the Divine, where they are able to see each other as God consciousness and to see the reflection of the other as being the mirror of themselves. They can understand that they are not separate. They are in fact, two parts of one being, especially during that moment of Sacred union, the merging of two becoming one. That two becoming one then creates three as we're able to conceive.

So it's raising the vibration, raising the frequency during that moment of Sacred union, dropping away the parts of the Self that are held on to emotional stories and past beliefs and leaving them behind. Understanding that they do not serve in this space and bringing the frequency, the vibration of Love as high as possible between the two who are in Sacred union. This is creating Temple space. This is allowing the calling in of us as a high vibrational being, as a high vibrational Soul to conceive into the human form into the Womb.

Birthing: These Souls are asking for Devotion to something greater, to welcome them as a higher vibrational being and be born in the same way they wish to be conceived.

Again, we wish to be welcomed. We wish to be honoured. We should be recognised for who we are. We wish to be born into Sacredness. We wish to be sung in on the voice of the Mother, the song of the Womb to guide us on our way down through the channel to birth.

Life: Devotion is an energy that is often bound to religion and being asked to Devote to something before it has been fully felt and understood, the dogmatic conditioning that "you will devote to this God as that's what we do", rather than open guidance to find the relationship within one's own self and from there feel and experience the Devotion. True Devotion is not something that can be placed upon you by others, it's not something you can be told to do. True Devotion comes from knowing the energy you choose to Devote to, creating your own relationship with it. From that place you can begin to understand that you are not separate and in fact, that which you are fully Devoted to is an aspect of yourself.

Exercise: Create an Altar to something you believe in, something you genuinely feel a connection to. It doesn't matter what it is, or what other people may think. Perhaps for you it's a God or Goddess, perhaps it's the ocean or your children. Choose a spot that won't be disturbed, even if it's inside your own wardrobe or a drawer. Place items that have meaning to you on or in that Altar. For me it's usually a nice fabric, some crystals, incense, candles and something that symbolises what I'm creating the Altar for, like a photo or statue. Start to create your own relationship to Devotion by visiting your Altar each day and tending to it, making sure it's clean, lighting a candle or incense and maybe even saying a prayer of your own making.

FOURTH GATE - INNOCENCE AND THE CERVIX

Clearing: Reclaiming Innocence is seeing the Innocence in oneself and being able to clear any blocks that have you believing that you are not pure, Divine Innocence. Bringing the body and the sexuality back to a home of Innocence allows you to heal the parts that you may believe have been taken from you or that have been conditioned into anything other than Innocent. The Cervix is also a bridge to the heart and as a woman activates and clears the Cervix she can expand the Innocence of the heart and of Love. The Cervix is also a gateway into the Lineage and Ancestral wounds, where they can be brought back to love.

Conception: With your beloved, seeing in their eyes the Innocence of who they are, the Innocence of their body and the Innocence of your Sacred Union. In Gate 3 you have already moved into seeing the Divine and now you can open more to the Innocence and connect in to the heart and start to merge from being two to becoming one. When you can open the fourth Gate, the actual physical Cervix can feel as though it's opening to receive the phallace (penis) deeper into the body and becomes more inviting to the sperm. In fact you or your partner may even feel like it's calling the sperm out of him and into your Womb.

Birthing: Giving the gift of Innocence as the baby passes through the Cervix allows them to embody that within their own field. Of course this is the Gate that must physically open in order for the birthing to even commence.

Working with the Cervix during childbirth can lead to a much more harmonious experience for both mum and bub. In fact, the opening of the Cervix can become an ecstatic experience for some women. As it is quite literally the start of the baby's journey into this world it can have a profound impact on their experience and view of the world.

Life: When you can begin to see the Innocence in others, a deep and profound healing can commence. What if you could begin to see the Innocence in the person who you perceive has hurt you the most in this life? If you could see that perhaps the things that have been said and done have come from the fact that their Innocence was shattered by another at some stage in their lives? Or that their lashing out or behaviour that is not acceptable has possibly come from their own inner turmoil over losing their Innocence? What if you could look in their eyes and see directly to the deepest part of them and find

59

the Innocence there? Perhaps you can't ever actually do that with the person, but I wonder what would change for you in your own life if you could allow yourself to see that in them. Perhaps it would also allow you to see that within yourself and reclaim your own Innocence.

Exercise: Journal prompt - when did you lose the connection to your Innocence? Who do you perceive was involved? Can you allow yourself to begin to look for the Innocence in them?

FIFTH GATE - LONGING AND THE WOMB

Clearing: As discussed in the previous section, there are many wounds and emotional stories that may be held within in the Womb. Here we choose to let them go, allowing the Womb to vibrate its life-force and begin to activate. One of the ways we know what the Womb wants is by connecting to her Longing. We have become so disconnected from Longing that it mostly shows up as its shadow, neediness, which is very often shamed in society and so we become completely disconnected from the depth of our Longing. To truly drop into the depths of Longing in the Womb can be confronting, and yet at the same time offers a new openness to following life's Ecstatic current.

Conception: If the Womb is Longing to conceive, allow yourself to own it, embody it and fully feel the Longing. When it comes to the Blue Diamond Souls they are asking to feel that you truly want them, that they are invited, however they are also very clear that they cannot come when you hold the energy of neediness. To own the Longing transmutes the neediness. The energy of neediness is like someone grabbing hold of you and pleading you to be there with them, and the energy of Longing is a deep invitation that magnetises you to them. Allow the Soul to feel your Longing as you consciously conceive them.

Birthing: A mother in the deep throes of labour is able to connect to the Longing for her child to birth into the world. The raw, primal state of a woman in the birthing dance with her child and her Womb is in her most Shamanic state, and the most transformative of initiations that she will experience in her life. Here she is able to connect to a place that is not available to her at any other time, when she deeply surrenders to the process. Her Longing will feel like it opens a new portal in her Womb, one where only her and baby exist in that moment, one where she would literally give anything and IS giving everything to her child as she finds a way to open her body completely.

Life: If you can move through the neediness and find the way to Longing, a new path of truth opens before you. No longer caught in the grasping for the mundane and instead cracking open to the Longing of life to move through you. No longer interested in the day-to-day actions and instead moved by an unseen yet deeply felt source that guides you in each and every moment.

Exercise: Place your hands over your Womb space, close your eyes and breathe into your Womb.

Imagine you can place your consciousness directly into your Womb and stay here for as long as feels intuitively right for the moment.

Then ask your Womb, "What are you longing for?" and listen for her answer. It may come to you as words, visions, feelings, or perhaps in this moment nothing appears.

If it's nothing, ask what's under the nothing (or whatever wording feels right for you).

If you get words, visions, feelings etc., be with those for a moment.

You may want to ask more questions like, "What do you need from me?" or "How can I support you?" or anything else that comes to mind that may help you to have a deeper understanding on what your Womb is Longing for, and perhaps how you can bring that into your life.

SIXTH GATE - SURRENDER AND CREATION POINT

Clearing: To Surrender to life does not come naturally for many people. Most are caught up in a tight web of control of their own fears and beliefs about life and what it takes to feel safe. Our Soul's purpose is found in the Sixth Gate, yet we need to be able to Surrender to something greater than what we can see with our own eyes in order to be able to truly connect to that purpose. To clear Surrender can bring a deep sense of freedom, to live beyond the need to control and instead stepping into the reality where we are divinely guided at all times. The freedom that comes when you can let go of the need to control opens up a profound sense of being connected to the greater picture, connected to the World Soul, deeply connected to the Womb and her Mysteries.

Conception: In natural conception we must Surrender to the things we cannot control. Will you conceive this month or not? Will you hold full term? Will it be a boy or a girl? When will you give birth? Conception is a path of Surrender to the greater order of things, realising the truth – that we are not in control. In the story I shared with you at the opening of this book, that was one of the most profound realisations for me. Here I was, a woman who was not looking to get pregnant, who was on a greater mission in life, yet the moment that Soul asked me, "Would you give everything for me?", there was not even a moment of hesitation and instead a deep and instant surrender to this Soul.

Birthing: I am not sure there is a greater Surrender than childbirth. I'm pretty sure every mother would agree. Surrender to when labour will start, Surrender to when the baby will enter the world, Surrender of the entire body, Surrender of all expectations on how it's all going to look. Ultimately the baby is the only one who knows the right moment to enter the world and so there is little choice but to Surrender to that. Even for women who plan a C-section you must Surrender your body to the doctors and realise you are not in control in that moment.

Choosing to dance with, rather than against, the Surrender in the birthing process allows the most easeful journey for both mother and child. Consciously working with this Gate at the beginning stages of birthing allows the following Gates the opportunity to fully activate naturally in each stage of birth.

Life: What would change in your life if you were able to Surrender? There are so many different layers to this question. Most people are so highly strung that their own nervous system is under constant pressure. If you can start to unwind that pressure in your body you will be amazed how much extra energy you gain. All the energy your body is using to keep you in control at all times is immense! The pressure that causes on your health is a big concern long term. If you are trying to conceive, this holding on in your nervous system is not doing you any favours.

Exercise: Journal prompt - what are you holding onto in your life that quite possibly is simply out of you needing to be in control, or out of fear of what would happen if you were to Surrender to the greater order of things?

For me to truly understand Surrender I chose to go to a Shibari (Japanese rope tying) session with a practitioner who I knew could hold a safe space for me to explore what it meant to Surrender. This may be a little extreme for you but it's an option for those who feel comfortable to push those edges.

You could choose to explore this with a partner or a friend and find ways that feel comfortable for you.

Perhaps even sitting between your partner's legs with your back against their chest and using your breath to Surrender back into them. See if you can start to match your breath to theirs and softly let go of any places you can feel your body holding on.

SEVENTH GATE - ECSTASY AND THE COSMIC WOMB

Clearing: Opening the body to Ecstasy is a profound way to live. Yet it makes complete sense that you should have full access to your unbridled life force surging through you in any given moment. Ecstasy is simply all of the cells in your body vibrating with life-force! Fully alive!

Is that not how we should all be living? Feeling fully alive and connected to the current of life force within us. Yet there are very few people in the world who are connected to this level of life-force. To clear this Gate opens you up to the full power of your Ecstatic being and opens doors to a completely new way of living. On page 41 I shared the story of following the Ecstatic current – that's how you can choose to live full time.

Conception: Connecting in to the Cosmic Womb at the moment of conception is the ultimate in conscious conception.

Birthing: For the Soul to fully land in the body it needs to be in Ecstasy. I've seen this over and over with clients and also in my time in the Mystery School. When the body vibrates Ecstasy, the Soul can take its rightful place and be fully present here with the body. During birth, if Ecstasy is activated in the mother's body, the baby's Soul is more likely to come through at birth. If it's not possible to activate within the mother at the time of birth, holding the baby against the skin and activating Ecstasy within the body with the intention of landing the Soul will do the same thing.

Life: You can choose to live your life fully connected to your own life-force and connected to the Ecstatic current of the Earth, moving through life with an entirely new level of connection to all that is.

THE COLLECTIVE WOMB

The Womb of the Collective consciousness is a pivotal aspect of conceiving the Blue Diamond Souls. As a collective, we need to work with and activate the Collective Womb to the vibrational frequency of 500 (love on Hawkins' scale of consciousness) to welcome in more of these Souls. All of my work, and that of the majority of people in my life, is to raise the consciousness of Humanity, this in turn will support the Collective Womb. If I can support as many individuals to release their past stories and trauma and activate their own Wombs, then we can work together to raise the vibration of the Collective Womb. We step beyond the personal focus and we start to look bigger at the "whole" picture, seeing that we are but one part of the full organism.

Whether you plan to have children or not, you would more than likely still be interested in the future of our planet and us as a Humanity (I hope). Together we can create a safe space for these Souls to find their home here and to ultimately guide us into the next dimensional state of being and away from possible extinction, which is what we seem to be hurtling towards.

Many women's Wombs are not able to hold the high vibration of the Blue Diamond Souls.

On a personal level this is where women who want to conceive can be focusing their attention.

We as a Collective of humans can all be working on the Collective Womb. To work more directly with the Collective Womb, whether you are interested in conceiving yourself, or you are interested in supporting the planetary shifts we are currently entering, will provide a more powerful platform for Humanity to birth ourselves into the next dimension.

The more we can work on the Collective Womb and raise its vibration the more easeful the arrival is for these Souls. The lower the vibration the more difficult it is for them to be birthed and also to live harmoniously. Imagine being born into a place where you can sense and feel EVERYTHING! The thoughts, feelings and energy of everyone around you, and then add on top of that the chaos that's happening on a global scale of people being controlled by fear and hate. The food, water and air being contaminated with chemicals that you can feel even before it enters your body. It's a lot to take in.

So, unlike most of you, where you are able to contain in your own space, we are not. We can sense and feel everything around. For example, as we sit here and you are asking me questions, I am doing my best to be present through this human form to give you the answers. This human body is now feeling a small sense of how we feel. Everything in 360 degrees.

Imagine if you now were suddenly placed somewhere with too much stimulus, very loud music, a lot of people talking, a lot of energy in every direction, a lot of lights, everything happening at once at very, very, very high speed. Imagine how that would feel in your system. How that would feel overwhelming and will be very difficult to move through your day if that is how you had to live, 24 seven. So, for a child, as you need to understand, most of us have not been in a human body before. It can be very overwhelming and feel quite extreme.

We can come together to make it as easeful as possible for their conception, birth and childhood.

These Souls are calling in community, asking us to step out of our insular bubbles of segregated living and realise that we are all in this together. Ultimately these children are asking to live in communities, to be around many different examples of people so they can truly grow and explore who they are. Often they are also not easy to parent and so the more community that can be around them, the more stable the growth environment is for them. It's not a coincidence that many communities are starting to form around the world, showing up as anything from Mystery Schools to groups of friends building tiny homes together on properties. I've witnessed these children in community spaces and they thrive! They come to life and they also bring the community into a space of Love, which is one of their greatest gifts to bring us. Keep in mind, we can make community anywhere.

THE COLLECTIVE FEAR

Fear and also hate, is a vibration that this planet, that Earth has been conditioned into. It's one that is very uncomfortable for us to enter.

This is part of why the pre work before many of us can arrive here to help is so needed. Because this vibration, this frequency of fear and hate, squashes and controls and has been placed upon you by organisations that you allow to control all of you.

69

What you need to understand is the energy of Love, the Love frequency, the I am presence of Love frequency, which is what Blue Diamonds souls are inherently coming to teach you is how to hold this frequency. Because when we hold this frequency there is no longer any such thing as fear and hate.

Yet for you to be able to care for that yourselves before we arrive, you need to start to raise your own vibration, your own frequency and to be able to step beyond, to be able to step above the energy that you are allowing to infest your body like an illness, it needs to be cleansed and released from your body and from your auric field so that you can raise your own vibration to no longer need to hold this frequency you call fear.

The conundrum we see is for us to be fully able to birth onto your planet in the way that it is done through the Wombs of the women. You need to release that fear and from your Collective Consciousness in order to be able to fully hold the frequency and vibration that we are, within the body. Yet, what we are coming for is to teach you to live a life that is of a different frequency. So, at this time, those of us who are not yet born into human form yet are in your dimension or in your realm, we are trying to assist you to understand how to move through these lower dense vibrations that many continue to hold within their physical body. Much of that is held and controlled from the low vibration foods that you eat, and the medications that are given – what you call vaccinations – that are given to your children to numb and capture them in a dense and low vibration and keep you caught in this constant cycle of unnecessary fear.

Yet those who run your countries in what you call Governments, the best way they can control and manipulate the world, the masses, is to continue to poison you through your water, through your food, through the air that you breathe. Through the medications that they force you to put into your children, especially those of us, the Blue Diamond souls who are coming through, and we appear different.

So how can you help the Collective Womb? You can work with your own Womb - that simple.

As an Activated Womb is a vibration and it transmits, then one Activated Womb can activate another. The more Activated Wombs we have the more the Collective Womb activates. You can also spend time with your own heart and finding the Love that goes beyond the personal level of Love that most of us live in, opening to find the ability to feel and follow Love as a vibration, and taking personal responsibility for own emotional reality and moving the lower vibrational energies from your field.

So, as an individual, when you experience the frequency, the vibration of fear which brings contraction, the best thing as an individual you can do is to find the self-responsibility, like housekeeping of your own body and your own energy field. There are many tools now available to you to learn or to find support on how to move that out of your physical denseness, as once it's held here in the dense, lower vibrations of your physical being, it's more difficult to release, yet not impossible, just more difficult and each of you needs to take self-responsibility to release these vibrations.

You may also consider taking your Womb connection to the Earth, Gaia, Pachamama. Keeping in mind that she is also holding the energy of the Womb. She is really the Great Mother, the one who is holding and caring for all of us. She provides us with everything we need (if we don't destroy it); oxygen so we can breathe, food so we can eat, water so we can take care of our bodies that are 50-80% water! She provides us with a place to live and ways to create shelter and homes.

Rather than ignoring her, which most people do, or going into the polarity of fear that she is dying, the best thing we can do is work with her. Find the ways you can cut down on your own wastage and the way you can live more in harmony with her and work on shifting your energy to vibrate WITH her instead of against her. If we are all energetic beings (which we are, by the way) then what we do with our energy makes a difference. If I hold fear that the planet is dying and I'm constantly sending her that fear I'm not helping! If I can move that fear through my own body and be responsible for my own feelings, then I'm helping.

If you feel she needs healing, other than the obvious of doing all we can in every moment to look at the bigger picture and make our choices accordingly, the best thing you can do is heal yourself. The fear that we are killing her really is pointless anyway. I mean, we are not killing her – we are killing the resources that allow us to live here. She will just keep on evolving with or without us.

As it's coming closer to breaking point (not the words I would usually use but I believe you will understand) for you as humankind, what you need to understand is people spend their energy and their fear worrying about the Earth and what you are doing to the Earth, and if she is okay. What you don't understand is She is fine. What you are doing is heading very quickly towards human extinction. There are many species that you are losing on your planet and if something does not change humans will follow.

If you start focusing on clearing and activating your own energy, stepping beyond the self, you can begin to see that you are part of an entire Collective, one small part of the bigger organism and connected to the World Soul. Then you can begin to see that what you shift for you, goes on and impacts the greater. You begin to see that even as only one person you do have the power to make change in the world, rather than get caught in the depth of overwhelm and helplessness that overcomes many of us when we look to the state of the World. From there you can connect into the Earth Womb and support her in the same way she supports us.

We can all choose to be part of the shift and change no matter where you are in your own journey.

ACTIVATING THE SEED

As with activating the Womb, we can also activate the Seed and the Phallic Gates of the man. I will touch on this teaching here by sharing a small section of a channelling session with the BDS about the seed. I have chosen to not share the full transmission as they are currently activating a completely new teaching in this area and I feel to honour that teaching and wait until they have downloaded the full teaching to me before I share the details. I believe this will be shared in the next book they are guiding me to write.

Q. What is the importance of the seed and what must men do to prepare for The Blue Diamond Souls?

In actual fact, we recognise that at one point you have asked this question before, we believe that was something along the lines of "what of the fathers?" and we expressed to you in that point, that the father was in actual fact not our highest priority. In that moment, the wording of the questioning was not there for us to be able to answer the aspect of the seed, of the sperm, which we are very grateful that you have recognised that this is in fact a very important path that needs to be shared and needs to be discussed.

Just as important as having the egg activated and in a state of vibrational frequency, in actual fact I believe you call it an Ecstatic vibration, where the cells are all vibrating together. It is just as important for the seed to be able to hold its own vibrational frequency. In fact the egg, as she vibrates, she magnetises, she calls the

75

seed that she is wanting to connect with, to work with, to combine with to become one, she magnetises and calls that seed or that sperm towards her. Yet it is actually the vibrational frequency of the seed of the sperm that allows the egg to surrender herself open to actually receive that of the seed. So both of them holding their own vibrational frequency together is the most potent and powerful alchemisation that you can create in order to provide us with the best possible chance at a high vibrational frequency DNA that allows our physical body to be birthed in a way that will give us the best possible opportunity to be able to move that particular physical body into a higher vibrational frequency. And as we are able to move our own body into a higher vibrational frequency, that is one of the ways that we are able to help support, guide and impact the vibrational frequency shift of those on your planet. So we want you to understand that this is a less travelled path, yet it is extremely important. Now, what is extremely important to convey to the people is that the healthy vibrational frequency of the seed is extremely important. And so as we have spoken about what it is that the woman is putting into her body and the vibrational spaces that she is in, it is very much the same for the men. The biggest difference here is that the seed, it is not like the eggs of the womb that are there for the duration of the woman's life. In actual fact, there is not as much work that needs to be done on clearing the seed as such, there is clearing to be done along the phallic gates. Yet the seed has such a fast regeneration, that in actual fact, there are not as many lineage codes that are stuck within the seed. However, there is still very much a need for the masculine counterpart, the male counterpart, to start to look at his generational line and to start to understand more about what it is that has been passed down from generation to generation, as those codes will be held within his seed even though his seed has a fast regeneration. In actual fact, it will continue to regenerate itself with the same codes and with the same information, unless he starts to look at what has been in that generational path along the line of men. And as with the women, back to seven generations, it is the same on the side of the men. In actual fact for him to do clearing along the line, along this generation of men, will start to make a difference for him and the quality and health of his seed, and can also start to shift the generational frequency that is passed from generation to generation through the seed.

So there is still work to be done around clearing in this area, yet different to the Womb — that tends to hold on to a lot of trauma and wounding and pain. The seed is different. It does not necessarily hold onto said traumas, but it does in fact hold on to a generational piece that it is important to be aware of and to consciously start to clear that path. So that in fact, the true vibrational frequency of the seed can be activated beyond the relationship with the men in the generational line, it can begin to be brought back to its ultimate light code frequency that is available to that particular man in this dimensional reality, in this lifetime.

PREPARING TO CONCEIVE A BLUE DIAMOND SOUL

If you are on the path of wanting to conceive a child (this is for both partners) this section is for you.

In a perfect world all children would be consciously conceived in Sacred space. This section is designed to give you a great start to that conscious conception path. If you desire to go deeper, you could check out The Conscious Conception Program.

Here are a few ways you can get started in your preparation.

Almost all of the Blue Diamond children who I have met, or who I know of, have been born to women with Activated Wombs, and all of them have been doing their own inner work. What's also fascinating is that many of these Souls have come to women who are not in the "trying to conceive" energy. They are relaxed and not attached to any outcome, and many are in fact a surprise and not a conscious conception at all – however, they are in a Sacred container of Love. I put this partly down to the fact they are not putting out a needy energy for a child to come and fill an empty space for them and partly because they are powerful and deeply connected women, so these Souls know they will understand them and hold the space they require as a child. They are women who are feeling "whole" within themselves and they are also not attached to "Mother" as a role they need to play.

So it is quite possible there are many BDS who have not been consciously conceived, yet they have known there is an agreement with that woman to birth them and they will come through anyway. As they are asking for a conscious conception and to fully support them, they have some requirements. It's most certainly a preference for them to be conceived consciously wherever possible, and actually for some, the process is one of the only ways they can come through.

It is predestined. We've already chosen each other. There's already a contractual agreement between Souls to support one another through this evolutionary change in humanity. It's now just a matter of those who will be guardians to us of remembering the agreement and the discussion with us.

For them to follow the agreed path of raising their own vibration to a level that is able to hold us, to birth us, to support us to enter, yet it also needs to be clear that when those who wish to call us in who are calling us from an energy of what you call neediness, an energy of grabbing for us, rather than opening and welcoming and allowing us, that we are unable to enter that space.

And so, we are choosing the ones who have already chosen us, but hoping that they remember, they re-awaken and follow the path that is necessary for their own preparation, in their own evolution, to be able to hold us and bring us through their own body, through their own vibrational field. For those who are able to "See", there is a Blue Diamond placed within the Soulstar of those who are to be birthing us through their womb. This is the way that we know how to find our way to them, is that Blue Diamond lights up when she is ready, when the Womb is ready and this is how we know that it is our time to birth through her. An important aspect that must be remembered here is that the two who merge in sacred union to create us are equally as important, as each provides the DNA imprint towards what our physical body will hold. However, also remembering that we are not attached to what you call Mother and Father.

So although we understand it may be confusing for you to understand the choice of who the father is, is not as high a priority for us as the Womb that we shall arrive through. Yet what is important to us is that His body also has a high frequency. That his body be also on an evolutionary path and that he is willing to be in an emotionally stable position, that if he remains in our life, to be able to hold that union with the bearer of the Womb, which you call Mother. We do not expect or need to come through a couple who will necessarily remain together, we are not interested in what you call marriage or the union of two needing to remain together.

What we are interested in is the vibrational frequency that they hold and that they are awake enough, aware enough to start to work with us rather than against us.

THE PREPARATION STEPS TOWARDS CONCEPTION

1. RELEASE CONDITIONING & RAISE YOUR LEVEL OF CONSCIOUSNESS

Holding onto old stories, conditioning, emotional patterning and old traumas keep you stuck in old ways of doing things –

outdated thought patterns that are no longer serving you and emotional reactions that are controlling how you show up in the world. These new Souls are deeply sensitive and can feel ALL of that in you, so the best thing you can do to support them (and ultimately you needing to live with them) is to clear those old patterns, take out the emotional garbage so to speak.

These children have such a different way of being in the world, the don't carry the same conditioning so you will be doing yourself a favour in being able to better understand them when you release your own conditioning as they are going to constantly be pushing up against those parts of yourself. They say children are a perfect mirror of all the patterns you run – wait until you see how intense it is with a Blue Diamond child.

What you need to understand is the Blue Diamond Souls, as we come in, we are different. We don't come through the preconditioning, I believe that's the correct term that you have learnt or absorbed from your parents and your grandparents. We don't understand that and we don't come in with that. We come in as a fresh being, not as a carbon DNA copy of the past. Because actually, our DNA is different. We, we are the start of a completely new human, a new humanity to help you shift out of the 3rd dimension that you all seem to be stuck in.

The most powerful tool I've come across for this is The Spiral!

Going through The Spiral shifted my reality and my world on such a different trajectory once I was free of all the shit playing out in the background. It's like having a computer with every single program functioning at the same time and they are all linked together somehow, so if one program doesn't like what the other one is doing, it all screams to a halt and no one knows why! Clear out the cache and all of a sudden, it's smooth sailing. It's the same thing with your emotional baggage. It's all playing out in the not-too-distant background - not only is that exhausting but it's also limiting your abilities in this life and squashing your level of consciousness.

These children are high vibrational beings and so the higher you can raise your frequency the more chance you will understand them more. The scale of consciousness as taught by David Hawkins shows us that we can vibrate at a different frequency which ultimately gives us a different view of the world.

Before we arrive, you need to start to raise your own vibration, your own frequency. Ultimately to be able to hold a base line of 500, which is love on the scale, will place you in a similar frequency to what the Blue Diamond Souls are here to shift humanity to. What you need to understand is the energy of love, the love frequency, the I am presence of love frequency, which is what Blue Diamonds souls are inherently coming to teach you is how to hold this frequency.

Basically I believe everyone can gain something in their lives from going through The Spiral and that every woman can step fully into her true Self by going through the Womb Spiral. In fact, if I'm totally honest I feel it's a big self-responsibility piece to clear your own field preferably before conception but at the very least during your child's early years so you can give them the best possible start of not being bound to your old conditioning, and to raise the vibration you and your family are operating from. It will also give you a better chance of understanding your Blue Diamond Soul child.

2. CLEAR THE BODY

As I mentioned before, in preparation for this book I took myself on a 7-day water fast – yup, nothing but plain water for 7 days! Why? I knew it was the most powerful way to clear my physical body of all the rubbish we put into it everyday. I don't eat junk food and still now after the water fast I can see so many places I was putting chemicals into my body that I'm just not willing to do anymore. A water fast is extreme so I certainly am not recommending that, and if you do please make sure you have the needed support. Not all bodies are made to fast and it can be extremely intense for some body types. Do, however, start to look at what you put in and on your body; every chemical and all the sugars are pulling your vibration down.

Find a good natural health professional to support you.

In preparation for us ensure also that your body, your energy field, your emotional body, your mental body and your physical body are all as clear of toxins as you possibly can, as this will give us the best opportunity, the best possibility of being able to carry to full term within the Womb and to be born into a healthy physical body.

3. CLEAR LINEAGE & ANCESTRAL LINES

As I talked about on page 38-40 we carry all the beliefs, stories and conditioning that our grandmother and mother passed on to us. Can you imagine walking around and literally carrying in a big bag on your back all the emotional baggage of both your mother and grandmother? Well that's kinda what you're unconsciously doing. Time to let that shit go!

It's not serving you, and most of all it will not serve your Blue Diamond child.

Check out some the free video in the bonus section.

4. LET GO OF FEARS

It's natural to have fears around conception.

Will I get pregnant? If I do, will I be able to hold it full term? Will everything be ok with the baby? Will I be a good parent? And so the list of fears goes on.

This energy of fear that I speak of is also a place when it comes to a couple choosing to or desiring to conceive us, is for them to move beyond their own fear of conception and realise that the energy of fear, like the opposite side of a magnet, is a repulsion to us. We are unable to come in close enough to conceive when that energy is present. And so, to do all you can to allow yourself to move out of the energy of fear and into the energy of Love. This will make it much easier for us to find our way into your Womb.

The conundrum we see is for us to be fully able to birth onto your planet in the way that it is done through the Wombs of the women. You need to release that fear and from your Collective Consciousness in order to be able to fully hold the frequency and vibration that we are, within the body. Yet, what we are coming for is to teach you to live a life that is of a different frequency.

And so, education is needed for especially parents and people who wish to be parents. To start to understand what it is they put in their own bodies and what it is they put in the bodies of their children. This can start to break the cycle. Yet those you call government won't make that easy for you, because they understand that then they will be forced into change.

Start to make friends with your fears, get to know them. Journal about them and find ways to let them go! There is a great resource to teach yourself clearing called Clear Your Shit by Dane Tomas, that is great for this.

5. HEAL RELATIONSHIPS

I am yet to meet a couple who don't have some history... someone hurt someone, life happened and caused issues, or just general day-to-day relating has led to some heartaches along the way.

You may have already "dealt" with them at the time. But did you actually? Or did they just get swept under the rug, squashed down, lost in the business of being busy?

It's time to get honest with yourself and with each other. I don't mean dredge up old stuff for the sake of it. I mean feel into what's still there? What have you moved past on the outside but truthfully on the inside is still a disturbance?

Take time together to share and to heal, to bring yourselves to a fully aligned place so your energies are moving together into conception.

COME INTO THE HEART

One of the big lessons these Souls are coming here to teach us is how to embody and vibrate the frequency of Love. Not the, "I love you because you love me", or the "because I have to love you" type of Love, but the I AM frequency of Love. In order for us to be able to begin to open to this level of Love we need to come into the heart and learn to move through the levels of Love.

The majority of people are living in the level of "immature" love, a love that is completely conditional. If you are the person I want you to be, then I can love you, but if you don't fulfil my needs, I can no longer love you. It's a love that's born out of fear, fear that you may lose something.

When we can move into the vibration of Love we can begin to literally follow Love. There are many people on the planet now learning to live in this place, yet it takes work to move through all those human fears that someone will leave us, we will be abandoned by Love. Following Love is actually the way we transmute the polarity of fear into Love, the way we open the heart more and the way we start to discover what Love actually is.

This is where you want to focus on your journey to conscious conception. How can you bring yourself and your relationship in a more genuine place of Love? Letting the reigns off the heart! Stepping into what one of my mentors calls WildLove. Loving beyond the boundaries and rules and being ALL in with Love.

The sooner we can move into this level of Love, the more we can begin to understand the Love vibration the BDS are here to activate in us. Yet first we must tend to our own heart.

As revealed by the Heartmath Institute, the heart has its own field, its own intelligence that can be read and measured. In fact, the heart often responds to stimulus faster than the mind does. They have done experiments where a person is placed in front of a blank screen and shown a series of random images. The heart will increase its rate before the screen flashes up the image of something scary and reduce it before it flashes up something like a child playing.

The field of the heart also creates what's called a Heart Wall. It's our way of energetically putting up a field to protect ourselves from being hurt. I've worked with countless clients on the Heart Wall and the results have been quite fascinating. Without fail, all of them are opening to more love in their lives and for themselves.

So if these Blue Diamond children are able to feel everything and that's the way they communicate with us, and the way we are mostly unconsciously communicating with them, it's about time that we drop the walls and the fears in the heart and allow them to deeply feel the truth of our essence rather than all the façades we put up.

Instant ability to read the thoughts of another and no need for words. Just need for energy and energy communication. Because of that sensitivity and our ability to communicate on that level, we are able to help those of you on a lower vibration to shift your own energy field as we are able to sense it and feel it in a different capacity than you can. Be aware of all the other

*ways that you are communicating with us all the time.
So, when you speak to us and for example, put a smile
on your face and say words that are supposed to sound
nice, but what you mean is something different. We hear
what is underneath.*

*We don't hear what is on the top, that you put in front.
So you may think that you're communicating with us in
a certain way, and we receive it in another because we
are constantly reading your field, your energy field and
reading your mind waves.*

6. RELEASE THE MOTHER/FATHER ROLE

One of the big pieces these Souls are asking for is probably
one of the most difficult. For you to let go of the typical
conditioning that's come along with the role of mother &
father so you can step into what they need of you, which is to
be their guardian.

*An important aspect that must be remembered here is
that the two who merge in sacred union to create us are
equally as important, as each provides the DNA imprint
towards what our physical body will hold. However, also
remembering that we are not attached to what you call
Mother and Father.*

*Parenting is a term, you need to understand that we do
not come to be parented.*

*And I understand this may be difficult for some hear,
but we are not interested in your constructs and your
terms that you call mother and father. We refuse to be
bound and tied to these terms. The truth is that you are*

there as our guardian to ensure that we are safe and to ensure that we have an environment conducive to our human form, our physical body growing old enough to be able to complete our mission here on earth. And so, those wishing to parent us, some find it very challenging and have a difficult time because we do not conform to what you expect. And in fact instead, we expect that you will learn to change and to respect our needs before your own.

If you think about it, mother & father come with a heaviness of old conditionings and beliefs.

Allow yourself to drop beyond the words and you may even find the freedom that comes with the release of these traditional roles.

Don't get me wrong, you birthed them into the world you will always be their mother, but drop the stories around it. Same for father.

7. CLEARING THE SPERM & THE EGG

If we want to raise the vibration of the Womb, we clearly want to do the same for the egg and the sperm, considering this is quite literally the blueprint for your child's future.

See also the section on Activating the Seed.

8. CLEARING & ACTIVATING THE WOMB

See the section on Activating the Womb.

CLEAR AND ACTIVATE THE WOMB GATES

See the section on Womb Gates.

9. CALL IN THE SOUL

If a BDS is preparing to birth through you, you more than likely have an agreement with them to do so. However, they need to know that you are ready, prepared for all that it means to welcome them into the world and that you are still maintaining free will in the agreement.

They will already be in your field so it's as simple as speaking to them and letting them know you want them, you are calling them in and that it's time! Don't worry if you cant feel or hear them as they can hear you.

Feel into what is the most natural way for you to call them in. Maybe it's doing a ritual, sitting in Temple space, calling them as you make love, writing them a letter or just simply speaking to them as if they are right there in front of you (as they probably are).

Let them know you are ready. Let them know how you feel, both the excitement and the fears. Let them know you want them in your lives. Welcome them in to your life. Share with them anything that comes to mind and heart.

> *We are able to move through different dimensions. Although it becomes very uncomfortable for us, we are able to shift down to your third-dimensional reality. Mostly, we can make this shift when we are invited through a Portal, an opening in the time space continuum and in the dimensions for us to be able to travel between realms.*

And so when these Portals are opened, it allows us to move from the 12th-dimensional plane into your third-dimensional plane and to be born into you as third-dimensional beings, humans. Yet, where we are from, our form is less physical, less dense, so we are able to move between time and space easily. So, although it seems confusing, we are already right here with you on this same planet.

CONCEPTION

PREPARATION

Even if you are not planning to conceive yourself, I believe you will find some interesting content here, either for your own journey or to support others.

The conception of a BDS is to be approached with Sacredness and with conscious intention. Creating a safe container of absolute truth, reverence, respect and honouring of the Soul you are calling in.

Imagine that you are inviting a high dimensional being into your heart and your home, as that is in fact what this process is. These Souls are requesting to be conceived in what they call "Temple Space". It is important to note here that Temple Space can look many ways so please do not get caught up in this and relax into creating what that means for you and your partner. For example you have read my Temple experience of calling in Souls at the beginning of this book. That is one extreme of creating Temple Space and yet at other times my partner and I will just light a candle to signify that we are entering Sacred Space. You cannot get it wrong! Just bring yourself into a state that feels Sacred to you.

Some suggestions may be to speak a few words of intention and love for one another, perhaps having a small note book that you write down an intention, lighting a candle, lighting incense, bathing and also cleaning the area, putting on some nice music, calling in any guides, saying a prayer, eye gazing or anything else that feels good to both of you.

You may wish to choose this moment to call in the Soul you are ready to conceive, or you may choose to do so at the point of ejaculation or spend a moment in the afterglow, or perhaps at all 3 of those moments. Perhaps they are words you speak out loud, maybe they are silent words you keep in your heart or you could write them down and keep them in a Sacred space like an Altar.

Trust that you and your partner will find the way that works for you! My partner and I have had moments where we put in all the effort to create Sacred Space, set intentions and prepare, but the pressure of the expectation puts one of us off and we end up just laying in each other's arms, or even allowing the pressure to build into one or the other's frustration. This isn't going to help the situation at all! Other times we've had fun with it and just whispered a few words right at the end. The important thing is to keep the lines of communication open between the two of you. Be clear each time you are approaching the fertile window and be clear if the intention is there to conceive this month or not! You are not baby-making machines and so human emotions and physical realities will come into play each month and they will all add up to bring a different experience forward.

When my partner and I were exploring if a Soul wanted to birth through us, or if it was here to guide this book and to guide me in how to help many couples conceive, we certainly journeyed a lot of emotional states together. One month we did conceive, however the implantation didn't take and I bled quite soon. It was emotionally a really difficult month to process the loss and when we came to the next fertile window I had to tell him I wasn't open to conceiving that month. My body was yelling at me to back off for a moment and allow it some recovery time. It's 100% ok to be all in one month and completely out the next month.

You may choose to set up Sacred Temple and intentional space once a month. Call in the Soul with a few words and that's it. That's totally ok too! Or you may prepare Temple Space every time you and your partner make love in the fertile window, or maybe for you that becomes what you do every time. Have some fun with it. Take the pressure off and use this time to learn more about each other, enjoy the ride. There are plenty of resources in the bonus material for this book that you may choose to use to give you some guidance and ideas along the way.

> *Also to remember when conceiving us, to welcome us and to call us in to fully let us know that now is the time that you are ready because although we can see the blue light on in your soul star when you are ready, we also need you to welcome us, to call us, to call us in and to let us know that now is the time that you are ready to be in a place to be able to truthfully hold us and all that we come with.*

> *Remember, to clear your own fear is to activate the Womb as we have previously told you about, to call us in to let us know that you are ready for us and to create as best you can a Temple Space or that of Sacredness as you perform the act of conceiving us. To remember to bring each other into Love, to bring each other into a space of the Love frequency, so that we can feel that frequency as we arrive into your Womb.*

If you have a community around you, who you trust and would like to bring into this journey with you, you could invite them to join you in a Calling in ritual. These Souls thrive on community and the offering of a collective energy calling them in is extremely powerful for them. This could be as simple as asking your closest friends to light a candle for you and hold the intention that a Soul will birth through you. The women may choose to bless the woman's Womb and the men may choose to bless the man's seed. You may even choose to make a full ceremony out of it. It's powerful and I have seen it work!

Can you even imagine how different the world would be if each person's Soul had been called in intentionally by a loving community? Would we have the same issues that play out in the world? I genuinely don't think we would. So many people are trying to fill a deep hole of feeling unworthy, unloved, abandoned and unwanted, that it is like a big vacuum sucking energy out of their lives. It's running in the background and silently controlling everything they do. Let's give the next generation the gift of knowing they are wanted, loved, worthy and deeply called for.

HOW TO USE THE WOMB GATES IN CONCEPTION

If you have deeply journeyed the Womb Gates this is where you can start to use them to guide the Soul into an Activated Womb. This is the most powerful path to conception and the activation of each of the Gates during conception and during birth gives the Soul a much stronger chance of coming through deeply connected to the body.

Make love through the opening of each Gate and as you fall through Gate 6 into Gate 7, the Man releases his seed into a fully receptive and vibrating Womb. If the woman has her Kundalini activated, as the seed is released, activate the Kundalini and allow the Ecstatic vibration of the egg to call in and open to the seed. In this moment call in the Soul, open to the Soul and allow it to become one with the energetic vibration that is being held in the love-making Portal. Dancing together in the Cosmic Womb, the three Souls start to remember and activate the Soul contract that has been agreed upon between you: Remembering that this moment has been predestined to happen at this moment, in this time, in this dimensional reality and here in the place of pure potentiality you have each realised this agreement into reality.

Through your own Activated Womb you become the Portal to the mysteries, the dancer of the cosmic realms and from here you are alchemising the mystery into current dimensional reality. You may wish to dance here in the Cosmic Womb for a period of time, allowing the annihilation of any mind space and simply exploring the expansiveness of time and space.

Here you may remember my story where I was asked, "Will you give everything for me?". From the place of surrendering the egoic self and floating in the space of annihilation, that is an easy choice.

If you have been blessed to have this experience, take time to gently ground together and allow any words that need to be spoken between you before you go on with your day as this is a powerful moment and may need witnessing to fully integrate.

DURING PREGNANCY

Remember that this pregnancy is a co-creation with the Soul that has chosen to birth through you.

Give yourself some time to begin to settle into the responsibility it is to birth and to guide this Soul into the world.

Start to find your birth support team who will understand what it is to birth a high vibrational being, calling in someone to support the birth who is sensitive to energy and, if possible, who is understanding of the Soul's path during birth.

Whether you are able to hear/feel it or not, the Soul is communicating with you all the way through the pregnancy and will let you know exactly what it needs. Take some time to listen, perhaps in meditation, gentle dance, quiet moments with your hands on your Womb and breathing together – whatever starts to emerge for you as your own natural way to communicate.

Of course during all pregnancies it's important to look at what you put into your body and what energies you are around. For these Souls the best start you can give them is to stay away from chemicals, low vibrational foods and unsupportive energetic spaces as much as possible.

We are most sensitive and to place such poison within our bodies, our physical form, makes it exceptionally difficult for our Soul and our Etheric, Energetic or Aural being to fully complete its mission here on earth.

And so, education is needed especially for parents and people who wish to be parents, to start to understand what it is they put in their own bodies and what it is they put in the bodies of their children. This can start to break the cycle. Yet those you call government won't make that easy for you, because they understand that then they will be forced into change.

Q. If I've chosen not to have children, am I keeping a Blue Diamond Soul from being born?

Well that just depends. So if it's already predestined, and we have an arrangement and agreement for you to birth a Blue Diamond Soul and then you choose not to have a child, then yes, you are stopping one of us from coming through. If, however, we don't already have one of those agreements with you, if you are not already predestined to birth one of us then no, you are not stopping one of us from coming through. So really, it's for you to journey deep within yourself and to remember, is there a connection to us? When you hear of us, when you read these words, is there something inside of you, is there a deep knowing, a deep sensation, a deep feeling that you are a part of us, that you belong connected with us that you are part of this journey with us? Then perhaps in actual fact you were predestined to give birth to one of us. However, if it more comes from a place of interest of where humanity is and in which ways you can support the birth of Blue Diamond souls and what it is that we are here to support in humanity alongside others, then perhaps that is actually your correct path.

If some reason we have a contractual agreement with a woman to birth through her Womb, and she either is unable or she makes the choice not to, which of course, we are always able to make a choice even if we have made a contractual agreement, either side of us is able to make the choice that it is no longer relevant.

Perhaps various situations have happened to either party and it is no longer a match for us to come through. So if for some reason, these contractual agreements need to be broken, we may not necessarily come through another Womb. We may choose however, to remain within the field, to remain within your dimension and to support and assist in every way we can without needing to actually be in physical form. We may choose to do so by remaining with the woman that we have the agreement with and supporting her in perhaps another area of her path. An example of this actually is the human that we speak through of this to you, we have been contracted to her, to birth through her, however, it has become clear to us that the best way that we can in fact work together is to currently provide this information through her. This is of higher importance and has higher value for the Collective than it is for us to individually birth through her Womb as one. And so, there are other women where perhaps similar situations may occur where we will remain in their field, where we will continue to guide and support them in the ways that they can support the rise in humanity and the shift in humanity. Or perhaps they may have something else that they are to birth into the world. Another way that they are here to support the shift and to support the change, in which case we will remain either with them or with the project or experience that they birthed into the world. Perhaps it is most important that our Soul remains with that to ensure that it is able to make the biggest impact in the world. In some cases, however, we may not be welcome anymore to remain in the field of that woman that we had the agreement with, in which case both parties can choose to separate, can choose to move on in our own ways. Some of us may in fact choose another Womb to birth through. Some of us, as I have said, may remain in the field to provide support without the need for a physical form.

CAN I STILL CONCEIVE A BLUE DIAMOND SOUL WITH IVF?

YES, absolutely you can. What's most important is that the preparation work is still done, the Sacred container is still honoured and that the Soul is still called in.

We understand due to many complications that oftentimes women are not able to conceive a child, much of this, we believe, is from the constant poisoning that is happening in your environment over a number of decades. And therefore the vibration is low and therefore more physical ailments are present within the Wombs of the women. Yet there are still ways that, if it is predestined for you to birth us, there are still ways that we can work together to ensure that we are still placed within your Womb for you to be able to hold us through pregnancy and to birth us.

What is important here is to still go through the preparation stages, to still prepare your own psychology, your own emotional body, your own energetic body and your own physical body, to prepare for us, to prepare for the conception and to prepare for the birth in the same way. It is also important that still the conception is done as Sacredness. We understand that through your, what you call IVF programs, that it can seem very clinical and very cold and very stark. However, there are ways and it is possible, if you are to start to look at where the rules can be slightly bent in your favour, to be able to be present

101

at the moment of conception and to be able to hold the energy of Sacredness between yourself and your partner, to be able to hold the energy of Temple and to remember that this can actually be done without needing to express to the others, that the ones who are more on the clinical side of things, you do not necessarily need to express to them what it is that you are doing, but to let them know that it is important to you to be present at the time and the moment of conception. And at that moment of conception, to still be calling us in, to still be letting us know that this is the moment that you are calling us to conceive. If for some reason this is impossible, even though we believe that there are ways that you would be able to encourage the bending of any rules that would make this impossible, if for some reason it is impossible, at least find out the moment in time that conception is going to take place and for yourself and your partner to go into Sacredness, to go into Temple space, if possible to go into Sacred union together at that moment when the conception would be happening in the more clinical environment, and to use your Shamanic body to understand that you are able to transport yourself to any place at any time. And so to use that Shamanic aspect of your being to be fully present at that moment of our conception, then yes, it is possible to use your system of which you call IVF to conceive us. We do, however, believe that many couples who have been led to believe that they may need this IVF procedure, that in actual fact if they were to go through the preparation stages of clearing their own bodies, and of activating their own Womb, and of releasing their own emotional conditioning, their own emotional past, we do believe that many of those couples who believe it is not possible for them to conceive naturally will find that it is now possible for them. We do understand, however, there are occasions where physically it just is not possible.

When you speak of surrogate. Yes, again, this is possible when you consider that what is extremely important to us is the Womb of the mother. This is one of the highest priorities for us, next step beyond the obvious of the sperm and the egg, as that will give us our physical support in this life, will decide our physical destiny in this life.

What is extremely important to us is the vibration of the Womb that will hold us till birth. So if a surrogacy is required, it is extremely important that this connection is created between the three. Between the Womb of the woman who would like to be able to conceive us and who is predestined, yet perhaps physically unable, between the man who will be the provider of the sperm to meet with the egg and also with the woman who will provide the Womb for the conception, and for all three parties to step into a place of Sacredness together, to step into the intention of consciously conceiving us and of calling us in. So in this situation, all three people are holding an equal point in the triangle. And all three people must be just as committed to the process of conceiving and birthing us as each other. In an ultimate world, were there to be a surrogate mother, there would be a deep loving container created between the three.

As remembering that emotional imprinting impacts us both in the Womb and when we are born, is remembering that the emotional as well as the mental agreement between the three must be clear. If this is not clear, you

103

will find that you will greatly be impacting our ability to complete our mission here on Earth, because we will be starting with an uneven vibration and within a Womb that is not there out of pure service, but has an emotional agenda.

TEMPLE & PORTALS

Throughout this book you have heard me mention "Temple" a lot, and also mention "Portals".

I feel it's best to let you hear about this directly from the BDS.

Q. What is Temple?

Temple is Sacred. Temple is a place of prayer yet in a different way to what many of you call prayer. It is a place of understanding that we are each the Divine, is a way of understanding that I can see the Divine in you, and you can also see the Divine in me. And that together, we can be the mirror for one another to remember that we are already the Divine, we are already God consciousness, we are not separate. So Temple is a space that reminds us, that allows us to remember who we truly are and connect into our God selves, to connect into that part of us that knows that we are all one Divine being. That we are all different expressions of the one. That we are, for example, all different Souls in the one body. Going to Temple is our way of remembering this aspect of the Self. Going to Temple is also the way that we activate the light grids and the DNA light codes of the planet. When we come into space together, we realise that each of us holds a different piece of the puzzle. That to sit alone and to try and activate grids upon the Earth for some, they hold just one key, but to bring many into the one space together, each holds their own individual key

105

and together you can activate the higher dimensional DNA light colour codes, the helix, helix of evolution, and that this can really only be truly activated in Temple. Yet each person who visits Temple must first journey through the individual path of dropping away the pieces of them that don't know that they are whole. The pieces of them that think that they are separate. This must be their first journey into Temple, the first level of the Temple. When they have experienced this aspect of the Self and they have been able to realise they are not separate, that in fact they are whole, is then when they can move on to the next level of the Temple. And this is where the magic begins. This is where the light codes and the grid activations are able to come into place. This is where each person is as much needed as the next. This is where we trust the greater order in things and know that it is not up to the individual to control or to manage what is happening. Yet it is to be in the space together and allow the energy to move, to trust the higher Divine order as each piece is put into place. By activating these DNA light grid codes, this helix throughout the Temples, this is where we can quickly raise the vibration of humanity, raise the vibration of this planet and raise the vibration of the beings on this planet.

This is why at this point in time you are seeing more Temples rise, we are starting to make our way into your dimension. There are more Temples awakening, this is all linked together as this is the time that you must now activate, so that we can rise together, so that we can shift dimension together. Because as we continue to remain in this three-dimensional space, we can see that we are heading towards the self-destruction of the human race. Yet when you can see from the higher dimensional realms that we are in, you can see that all we need to do is shift the vibration, shift the frequency, raise the level of consciousness of this planet, of the beings of this planet, and that is done through Temple. When you move through this second level of the Temple, we come to the top, to the point of the Temple. I need to check if, if I am allowed, if I have permission to share with you actually what the top of the Temple is for, because in actual fact, humanity is not yet at the level of reaching the top point of the Temple.

There are beings on your planet, not only us as Blue Diamond Souls, but other beings who are on your planet who are working to bring many of you up to the place of being able to reach this top point. Yet, there is still more work to be done. And so at this point in time, I have been advised that I am not to share what happens in the top of the Temple, but that as a human race for you to start to understand the importance of Temple and to bring as many people as possible through the first level of the temple as quickly as possible and as soon as possible. It is an imperative part of the shift of humanity, as well as the arrival of us, the Blue Diamond Souls, working alongside you to shift this vibration together.

And as you bring many people into this second level of the Temple, those who have already been working in what you call this lifetime with the Temples, they are then able to more easily shift up into the second level and to really remain in that space to truly work their magic together. It is already happening on this level, but it needs to happen more.

And once they are in this space, then it is possible to share what happens at the top level of the Temple. We recognise that perhaps for many, this is too advanced.

We do not wish to perturb you and turn you off the Temple by going into such advanced technology. And so it is important that you understand that you can also, even as an individual, take yourself into Temple, you can take yourself into Sacred space. You can take yourself into a journey of releasing and letting go of the parts of yourself that do not think that you are whole, that do not think that you are part of a greater organism. And this you can do as an individual, you can raise your own vibration, your own frequency by making choices about the people that you are around and making choices on the way you treat your body and what you put into your body to raise your own vibration, your own frequency, and to shift your own emotional intelligence by releasing past conditioning, by releasing past stories and beliefs that are no longer serving you and holding your vibration down. Just by stepping into that level of Temple you can begin the journey and you hear us speak about how we are calling out to be conceived in Temple space. What we mean by this is for the couple who are merging in Sacred union, to be coming to this place together, where they are able to see each other as the Divine, where they are able to see each other as God consciousness and to see the reflection of the other as being the mirror of themselves. They can understand that they are not separate. They are in fact, two parts of one being, especially during that moment of Sacred union, the merging of two becoming one. That two becoming one then creates three as we're able to conceive.

So it's raising the vibration, raising the frequency during that moment of Sacred union, dropping away the parts of the Self that are holding on to emotional stories and past beliefs and leaving them behind. Understanding that they do not serve in this space and bringing the frequency, the vibration of Love, as high as possible between the two who are in Sacred union. This is creating Temple space. This is allowing the calling in of us as a high vibrational being, as a high vibrational Soul to conceive into the human form in the Womb. So, it's important to understand that there are many different dimensions, many different layers of the Temple.

And that is what you may call a lifelong journey, that it is even beyond just this Soul incarnation. That journeying through the Temple is part of our constant evolution and constant understanding of how the greater picture works and of how we fit into the greater picture and of seeing how the whole dimensional matrix moves as one.

Q. How do these Portals open and how do we call you in?

We find your question amusing because you already know the answer. However, we understand that you ask the question for others, not for yourself. To open this Portal is to journey to the Cosmic Womb, to the Void, the place of pure potentiality. This is the closest that you have to reaching our dimension. This is the closest meeting point between the realms.

So for you to journey to the Cosmic Womb, and to call us, to simply welcome and call us in with Divine pure intention.

The more of you that gather together at once to hold these Portals open, the more of us can come through to support you as humanity. And so, when done in community space, togetherness space, and each bringing yourselves to the Cosmic Womb, together as one Collective, as one organism, not as a group of individuals, but as one organism, that vibration becomes strong enough to create a Portal that opens for long enough and magnetises many of us in. Yet also as individuals, as two merging to bring us through you can still do the same and move together to the Cosmic Womb. Yet, it is important to know that this is not as powerful. Once a Portal has been opened that is large enough to bring through many, then as the individual couple it becomes easier to just tune in and tap into the fact we are already in your dimension. So once again, to go to the Cosmic Womb yet understanding that we are already in your dimensional realm.

So allowing those whose purpose on this earth is to hold the Portal open for us, allowing and supporting those who understand the way to do this, so that then the individuals can more easily call us in to conceive.

BIRTHING A BLUE DIAMOND SOUL

Q. How do we know if we have birthed a Blue Diamond Soul or if a woman is pregnant with one?

When we are born look to our eyes and in our eyes you can see that we are not a baby. In our eyes you can see that we are a higher, Divine being, who is presenting itself in physical form as a baby. Oftentimes the mother will feel, if she is in tune enough to frequency, she will be able to feel when we are in her Womb. It's a knowing, it's not an instruction we can give.

Q. How do Blue Diamond Souls want to be birthed into this world?

Thank you for asking. Again, we wish to be welcomed. We wish to be honoured. We should be recognised for who we are. We wish to be born into Sacredness. We wish to be sung in on the voice of the mother, the song of the Womb to guide us on our way down through the channel to birth. Understanding that during the birth process is the moment that the Soul is able to fully connect to the body to the human form, to the child.

So understanding the importance of this process of birth to truly call us in. Sing us in. Welcome us in and let us know that all of us are welcome. That the Soul is being called into this body at this moment in time to be born.

This is able to be done with the voice of the mother, with the voice of the Womb. It is also able to be done through opening the pathway down through the mother from the Cosmic Womb, down, down, into her Womb. I believe you call it... I see it as images, as 7 lights (the Womb Gates), calling us down through that channel, guiding us to ensure we understand that you are ready. You are welcoming us. You are singing us into the Sacred space to the Sacredness with devotion, with reverence. We understand that for many of you, you go, words are hard sometimes – go to the place with the lights. How many of you go to the room with the bright lights?

Wait I need to ask the human, ask the human, let her do that. How many of you need to go to the hospitals in order to be able to birth your children, as this is the way you've been conditioned to believe that it needs to be done? Yet wherever possible, we ask that you stay away from the bright lights (Hospital), that you stay away from the hands of those that are unknown, from the energies and the vibrations of that which are unknown.

That you keep us in the space that is known to you, preferably within your own sacred Temple, your own home. Preferably to birth us into the space of water, knowing that we are mostly water, for us to come into that vibration, that frequency of water is where we feel the safest, where we feel the most welcomed and where we feel the most at home, and where the entrance for us into your world is less, less impactful upon our bodies. As we've shared with you many times we are very sensitive, and arriving with sudden impact and bright lights, into the hands of people who you do not know, and who's vibrational frequency is unknown– this is very confronting for us. So bringing us into a space where you are in more control of the frequency and the vibration of that room is where we feel safest to arrive and where we can come in more of our fullness, in more of our wholeness. Knowing that it is safe to be here in this dimensional realm. The reason we speak before of the song, the mother's song and the song of the Womb, is again to allow us to feel your vibration, to feel your frequency from the inside of your being, the inside of your body, to use your voice to guide us on the way through and out of your Womb. Also being highly aware of whose hands are placed upon us first.

And knowing and understanding what is the vibrational and emotional frequency of this person who places their hands upon us first, who places their energy imprint upon us first. Recognising that this will drastically impact how we move in the world and how easily we are able to navigate our way into your dimension, how easily we are able to settle in and understand what it is to live in a three-dimensional body. Keeping us away from other influences, away from other energies, away from other emotional beings, away from other low-density energies for at least the first three days.

Keeping us in places with dim lighting, soft, soft energy and safety allows us to spend time to get comfortable in this three- dimensional, low-density body, easing us in. That way we know that we are safe and there is less shock involved in our arrival because although we have an arrangement and agreement with you, to birth through you and to come into your three-dimensional realm, we have not yet experienced it. So it can be quite a serious shock to us on arrival, and so keeping that awareness in mind at all times allows us to have a more peaceful journey in.

113

Ensuring that those you choose to surround yourself with at that moment in time, that you trust their Love vibration, that you trust that they are there for the higher good and not for personal gain. Remembering at all times that you are birthing a high vibrational being, a high frequency being, will allow you to set the best environment for us.

Q. What happens to you if that can't happen – say because of trauma, caesarean, or low vibration environments?

We go into contraction. Going into contraction and fear in the body and it's more difficult for us to bring the full vibration of our Soul through. It's possible during that type of birth that we may not fully bring in our Soul into that body as it may not be able to hold it. The lower vibration, the lower density body might not be able to hold the full frequency of our Soul. And so it is possible during traumatic birth that we may only bring part of our Soul through and hope that someone around us is able to, at some point recognise this for us and to help guide us to bring our full Soul down into our body at a later stage. So if we are born into a situation that we understand happens in human form, often does, do not despair that you have done something wrong for you have not done anything wrong, this is the way of things in your dimension. It just is how it is, so please do not buy into the fear that you missed the Temple. In that moment do all that you can to ensure that, if not at least the mother, that somebody else in the room is able to be calling us in, is able to be singing us home, is able to be showing us the way and letting us know that it is safe to come. This does not have to be the mother if she is in distress. Her focus must be on the physical dimension, the physical realm to ensure that both her and the physical body of us as we come out, is kept safe.

Yet she can have a Soul Midwife with her, she can have one with her who understands how to support us and guide us through. When it becomes most important is post birth in this situation, is important that as soon as possible mother and child are placed together. The body is able to feel the vibration and the frequency of she who birthed her/him. To have this reconnection to feel the body allows us to drop out of contraction, come back into fullness, to feel her breath, to feel her heartbeat, to feel her vibration, to feel her song. She can still sing us in even after the physical action of birth. And again, during the three days after birth, to keep us in low light, low stimulation (the least stimulation possible) environment is what can serve us best in that time, especially if the birth has been traumatic.

If someone is present who understands how to work with energy in that situation, it's best to also ensure that our own etheric field is clear of obstruction and that we have not had energetic tears during the experience of the birth process, that our energy field is intact, this is of high importance to us. So to ensure our best possible opportunity at growth is to help us to maintain our energy field as soon as possible after birth. If for some reason we have been separated, separated from mother, not placed skin to skin, we have been separated during the birth process and touched by the hands of others who do not know their emotional intelligence, their vibrational frequency, ensure that is reset to the mother as soon as possible. So to spend as much time as possible skin to skin with mother for the three days following will help to reset the imprint that has been placed upon us by somebody else. Also understand, we can communicate with you. Immediately we can communicate with you from the Womb, we can even communicate with you before conception. We can communicate with you, right from the moment of birth. All you need to do is to listen, to hear us, as we are able to send you mind waves, frequency vibration, and communicate with you constantly to tell you what it is that we need. So it's important to just listen.

BLUE DIAMOND CHILDREN

The BDS have a lot to say about who they are and how we can best support them.

Q. And so you arrive as children to wake us up – how can we better understand which children are Blue Diamond souls so that we can help you? Is there a way to know if someone has a Blue Diamond Soul?

Yes you can see it in their eyes. You will be able to see from the moment a child is born in their eyes, they are awake, they are not asleep. They have a clarity in their eyes. And it is as though an adult is looking out to you from the baby's eyes. Because it is a high vibrational, highly intelligent Soul, not a baby. So for many you will be able to see from the moment they are born if you have not already been aware whilst they were in the Womb.

Many women will be in tune enough to be able to feel from the moment of conception or from the pregnancy that she in fact is holding a Blue Diamond Soul because this soul will be communicating with her. She also may notice that within her own body she is suddenly eating very differently. She suddenly is unable to eat low vibrational foods that have been poisoned that she is more focused on high vibrational clean diet. This also may be an indication that she is pregnant with a Blue Diamond Soul. I believe we have also shared before that these women hold a Blue Diamond energy within their own Soul star. So for someone who has the gift of sight they may perhaps be able to see this Blue Diamond within her

Soul star so then when she conceives they will be aware that it is a Blue Diamond. So when we are born, as we say, it is often by the eyes or it will also often be able to be told by the fact that we, for someone who is sensitive and is able to feel vibration, that we feel different. We are not like other children, we have a different vibrational field, perhaps someone who is sensitive to energy will be able to tell in this way, someone who is given the gift of hearing will be able to hear us communicating with them immediately and we'll be able to ask us themselves if we are in fact a Blue Diamond Soul and what it is that we need in order to be supported as such. As children, you may be able to tell, you more than likely will be able to tell who we are by a high sensitivity. The sensitivity may appear different in every child, we know we have talked about this sensitivity many times, but it is one of the easiest ways to be able to recognise who we are. We may be highly sensitive to spaces, to people, to different lighting, to different music. It's part of our gift and yet also can feel at times like part of our curse, because those around us do not always understand. And so you can tell if your child is perhaps highly sensitive to energy, at times repulsed by different people and at times attracted to different people instantly, or is exceptionally fussy around what they choose to eat.

What they are willing to do with their time perhaps may seem like a very difficult child. Because there is high demand of our environment being held to a certain standard.

You also will find that we are highly intelligent even as young children. This, if encouraged may show up in all different forms. Yet, if it is not encouraged, you may perceive that in fact that we are the opposite. You may perceive that in fact we have learning disability or social disability. But this is actually a reaction to the environment more than what it is our actual truth. As we get older, to the time when you would normally send your children to institutions, you will find that it is difficult with us because we are not suited to your current system.

And so you may find that you send us to school and we are sent home, or that they are not well-equipped to be able to care for us in the way that we need. But always remembering that you can communicate with us psychically and energetically and we will tell you who we are. We feel like it is obvious. Yet we understand that sometimes because you are also numb to your environment, it may not be as obvious to you.

Q. How do we know if we have birthed a Blue Diamond Soul or if a woman is pregnant with one?

When we are born, look to our eyes and in our eyes, you can see that we are not a baby. In our eyes you can see that we are a higher divine being, who is presenting itself in physical form as a baby.

Oftentimes the Mother will feel, if she is in tune enough to frequency, she will be able to feel when we are in her Womb. It's a knowing, it's not an instruction we can give.

Q. What qualities does a Blue Diamond child have?

Because our vibration is a much higher frequency than you are used to experiencing on your planet, that shows up as a high sensitivity to being able to feel and sense everything around us as if it is us, because we live in a reality where we see that we are all the one organism

119

expressing different parts of itself. And so, as children, we may be confused with children who you call autistic, and who you call, I believe, ADHD or other other names that you may call these children who appear different and extremely sensitive to the world, to sound and to senses. Because we feel and sense all vibration. So, unlike humans, where you are able to contain in your own space, we are not. We can sense and feel everything around. For example, as we sit here and you are asking me questions, and I am doing my best to be present through this human form to give you the answers. This human body is now feeling a small sense of how we feel. Everything in 360 degrees, she (this Human I am speaking to you through) is able to sense the emotions and the thoughts of every being present in this space. So, for a child, as you need to understand most of us have not been in a human body before, it can be very overwhelming and feel quite extreme. So perhaps we need to be kept in different spaces or treated differently, spoken to differently as we learn to adjust to life in a human body. As that human body grows, we are then able to start to use that sensitivity as our gift, which it is, and to teach the rest of you how to start to access those gifts for instant manifestation. We have instant ability to read the thoughts of another me and no need for words. Just need for energy and energy communication. Because of that sensitivity and our ability to communicate on that level, we are able to help those of you on a lower vibration to shift your own energy field as we are able to sense it and feel it in a different capacity than you can.

Also, because time is new for us, when we arrive in human form on Earth, we may not understand as a child the construct of time, the limitations of time. So when you tell us to be ready in five minutes, this means nothing to us. We don't understand the way you communicate this phenomenon because it doesn't exist for us until we arrive in your dimension. Yet, as we grow older that also allows us to assist in seeing what's happening on your planet from a different level. To not be stuck in the way you see it as linear, but to understand that we can change time, we can bend, we can bend time so therefore, we can change things in what you would consider to be the past, to impact the current or what you would perceive as the future.

That allows us to be able to shift the direction of the planet on your timeline to possibly be able to help you not reach the place of extinction of your species. We also communicate differently. So, as a child, it may seem very difficult to get us to communicate with you in the way that you expect. Because this is not how we communicate. Be aware of all the other ways that you are communicating with us all the time. So, when you speak to us and for example, put a smile on your face and say words that are supposed to sound nice, but what you mean is something different. We hear what is underneath. We don't hear what is on the top, that you put in front. So you may think that you're communicating with us in a certain way, and we receive it in another because we are constantly reading your field, your energy field, and reading your mind waves. Yet again as we grow older and learn to be in this human form that allows us to see beyond the façade, the fakeness of the leaders and rulers of the countries that as humans, you all seem to blindly follow and believe. So we are able to see beyond that and to understand the truth and therefore help and assist you to make the changes necessary.

It is also very normal for us to communicate across dimensions and to be able to see what you cannot

121

see. So as children, it may seem like we are talking to invisible beings. What you need to understand is they not invisible to us, they're just invisible to your limitations. To us they are very much real, as much as you are, and sometimes we see that this causes confusion and fear in the adults who are what you call "parenting" the Blue Diamond Soul children. Parenting is a term, you need to understand that we do not come to be parented.

And I understand this may be difficult for some to hear, but we are not interested in your constructs and your terms that you call mother and father. We refuse to be bound and tied to these terms. The truth is that you are there as our guardian to ensure that we are safe and to ensure that we have an environment conducive to our human form, our physical body growing old enough to be able to complete our mission here on earth. And so, for those wishing to parent us, some find it very challenging and have a difficult time because we do not conform to what you expect. And in fact, instead, we expect that you will learn to change and to respect our needs before your own.

Q. How can someone be a good parent to a Blue Diamond Soul?

First there is pre work to be done. First is for them to shift and change their own vibration of their form and of their Auric field. To release past traumas, to release past fears and become self- responsible, to move that which you call Ancestral time lines, where you have carried those stories from your own parents and their parents, is to take self-responsibility, to release those from your field and to change your understanding of the Womb. Shift the frequency and to raise the vibration of the Womb to be able to conceive us and to be able to carry us to full term and give us the best possible start is to be held and housed within a physical body that is clean. That does not contain the poison of the food and the water and the medications that are so heavily on your planet.

Once we are born, the best way you can support us is to understand that we are a powerful being and a powerful Soul living a baby's body, that we are not a baby. To start to understand and respect that we are coming here as teachers and that we have chosen you to be able to be our guardian and to realise the honour of that. Really your role is to keep us safe. To ensure that we are not infected with what I call illnesses of low vibration, emotions and energies, and that we are not infected with the poisons of your food and your water. Understand that we will be very different to you, that we will be very different to any other children that you may have had before, for each of us that appears differently. But to keep in mind and always remember our sensitivity and the different ways that that may show up and to not try to make us wrong for those, and to not try and impose your construction on us. Allow us to breathe and the space to experience freedom, in our own expression, and we fully understand that at times that is not easy. And we hope you understand that you have been blessed as being the guardian of the new Humanity, that you are not a parent to a child. That you are part of the change. And we believe when you see that you are part of the change, that you will adjust your own viewpoint. Do all you can to understand us more. Realise that you can communicate with us. We can use words with you from the moment we are born. If only you ask us and you listen, and you understand that we are not restricted by the need to speak the words out loud, that for us it is a vibration. And we can tell you at all times, what it is we need if only you would take the moment to ask us and to listen and to be conscious of, when you are around us, what is happening in your own energy field and what is happening with your own emotions. We do not expect you to not experience emotions. We understand this is a human phenomenon. But what we do expect is for you to hold the self-responsibility around your own emotional state and to be in a state of honesty with that. For the moment, that's all I have for you on this.

Q. How do you prefer to be parented and raised?

We expect to be given respect, we expect to be supported.

We expect that those who are guardians to us will be taking responsibility for their own energy, for their own environment and for the environment that we are being cared for in. We ask, we struggle with the word "parented". As I've shared with you before, we ask that the guardian, or guardians, do all that they can to provide us with the freedom to express our own truth of who we are. To understand that at times, our needs will be very different to their other children and to do their best to understand and support us through that.

We also understand that you are caught very often with your own conditioning, your own beliefs and your own rules that you are stuck within. We also understand that sometimes "parenting", as you call it, us in the way that we require may not be easy. So, we ask of you to be as open and honest with us as is suitable for our own level of development. For example, it is okay to tell us that you are confused or it is okay to tell us that you don't know how to give us what we need. It is okay to work together with us, rather than be expected to know everything yourself.

Remember that for most of us, it is the first time in a third- dimensional body. So we are also still learning how to fit into your lives and yet also to advise you on what our needs are. But the highest need is that you are open, that you are open- minded, that you are willing to grow with us, that you are willing to do your best in each moment to lovingly support us and our needs, knowing that we have a mission and a purpose here. For example, I see many, as I have spoken before, I see many young children stepping up and speaking in the world around environmental issues. When you see that your child has something similar, perhaps environmental issues or technology or bringing Love to the world, when you see this start to appear in them, do everything you can to support that. Do not squash it. Even if you do not understand it. Do your best to be supportive and work side by side with us. Please do not shut us down. Please also watch out for the environments that we are in. Being aware that we are sensitive to energies, trying not to have us sleeping in rooms with technology, and if for some reason we do need to be in a room that has, for example a TV or a computer, please ensure that it is switched off before we go to sleep, and that we spend the least amount of time possible around your electrical devices as this will impact our energy field and will impact our ability to continue to do our mission here on Earth. It will also impact the way that we navigate life and the way that we show up in our relationship with you. So if we are playing out perhaps this is one of the areas to look to. The other is what poisons are being put into our bodies, is keeping your eye out for not having us injected with vaccines and not feeding us with sugar and not giving us high-preservative diets, but doing your absolute best to ensure that our bodies are clean as this will also impact our emotional and our mental bodies, and will impact the

125

way that we are able to communicate with yourself and with others because we will go into unusual emotional behaviours or unusual mental patterns. And this is often from what we have been putting inside our bodies or the environment that we are are in, often the quality that we are in, the quality of the water that we drink. It's just, do your best to ensure that it is as clean living as possible.

Q. How can we best support Blue Diamond children, helping them to reach their full potential?

Thank you for asking this very important question. As we have mentioned many times now so we know you understand we are highly sensitive. First and foremost is to actually begin to understand what that might mean. Imagine if you now were suddenly placed somewhere with too much stimulus, very loud music, a lot of people talking, a lot of energy in every direction, a lot of lights, everything happening at once at very, very, very high speed. Imagine how that would feel in your system. How that would feel overwhelming and would be very difficult to move through your day if that is how you had to live, 24 seven. For us, everyday life can feel that intense and so do all you can to keep us in environments where the energy frequency is comfortable for us, where the lighting is comfortable for us, the sound levels are comfortable, that people that we are surrounded by feel comfortable. You will be able to tell very quickly if we are not comfortable by our behaviour and the way we move in that small body, perhaps by making a lot of noise or what you may call "misbehaving" or needing to escape and hide. Rather than see these as negative behaviours that are being played out, understand that they are coming from an over stimululation from somewhere and have a look at where you can help to maintain and shift that stimulus for us.

126

Look to things like lighting, temperature, sound and energy. Look to each of those things and try to shift and see what might change for us. Perhaps, even in some circumstances, being out in a noisy environment might be as simple as placing headphones on the child and playing something that they find relaxing, that is able to calm the body, because they are not only hearing the sounds, they are also feeling them penetrating into their body, as well as constantly feeling everything on an energetic frequency. This does not mean lock your children away.

Quite the opposite. We like to be around many different adults and to understand and to learn from many different adults in spaces beyond where just the parents are. But just being aware, when our behaviour shifts, of what that might be about. Also supporting what it is that is placed into our bodies and onto our bodies, ensuring that we are not being poisoned, that our energy field is not being poisoned as this will cause us extreme discomfort.

When parenting us, try to understand that although we are in a small body we are highly evolved Souls, so talking to us like we are different to you, like we are not as intelligent as you will not help us, talk to us like we are another intelligent being because we are. Ask us, as you would another intelligent being, what it is that we need or how we can best be supported.

Do the best that you possibly can to be responsible for your own emotional intelligence and your own emotional frequency. This does not mean do not show emotion and try to block your own emotions. It just means to be self-responsible for what is moving through your own body and to allow those emotions and those frequencies to move. Because when you hold them within your own body, we then feel them and we may perhaps play them out back to you. Because it is in the field, it is in the space and it needs to move. So, if you do not take responsibility to move it, then we may well move it through our bodies, reflecting that back to you. And you may then blame us for that, which was actually your own internal experience that you had not taken care of, that we needed to be responsible for it for you. So being punished for such behaviours feels very out of alignment for us. As we get older, start to consider what it is that we necessarily need to be able to grow our own skills for what we are here on this planet for. Perhaps that does not fit into your organisations (School), where most of your children go and sit and learn the same thing side by side, side by side every day, same thing. No matter what their purpose or their path is. They go and they are numbed and treated like robots. We are not robots. We are usually not comfortable in that environment.

Unless it is with adults who understand how to guide us into blossoming, how to guide us into learning, how to guide us into bringing our physical being into a state that is able to express our Soul's purpose in the world. If you squash, and numb us, we cannot do what we are here to do. It is only with loving guidance and support, to continue to grow and learn and to continue to do our mission, that we are able to truly support Humanity. We are not here to go into your corporations and work your jobs. We're here to make a rapid shift for humanity. And so when it comes to our education, treat us in that way. Do not send us down the conveyor belt into a place that will just shut down who we are and our gifts, as that is a waste of calling us into your planet.

Q. How about Education?

We are not made for your current institutional system. It does not support our growth. It does not, in fact, support the education that we need to continue to tap back into our own intelligence. In fact, it does the opposite and so we believe that there are already many in your dimension who are trying to make a shift and a change in your educational institutions, because they are starting to see and be aware that we do not respond accordingly. Wherever possible, send us into spaces that are supportive of us choosing our own learning path, of us having the freedom to explore, not of being taught only what is the cookie cutter system for every single child. This does not support our growth. So we see that, as soon as possible, shifts and changes need to be made in your educational system. We see that people are now more often home-schooling, educating from home. This is a fantastic start to making the shift and making the change. But also, the highest way for us to learn is to be together with others like us, because when you place us together, our energy feeds off one another and we build our own intelligence much faster. And this way, we are able to start to network our energies and network our minds and create a bigger and faster impact. So although we are extremely grateful for those who have been able to use the resources to give us home-schooling, and we see that that is currently by far the best option available, we also highly encourage those who have the ability, the resources and the skills to start creating spaces, educational spaces for us to learn, for us to inspire, for us to grow together. Because as we grow together, we can make a bigger impact sooner. When we are born into spaces with others like us, we start to realise and remember that we are not alone. If we are kept completely separate, we can sometimes go into what you call "depression" because we feel overwhelmed that there is only us and we need to remember that there are actually many of us here. And so when you bring us together in spaces, like that, for example, you put 2 into a room together, the energy that will create will be 4, you put four into a room together and actually the energy we create will be of 12 people. So the more of us, the greater magnitude, the bigger difference we can help to make and the faster. So wherever possible, work against the current institutional schooling system and find ways to place us into a system that has more freedom and more support.

You will discover that in actual fact, our intelligence will grow tenfold of what it would if you were to numb us and place us into a school that to us feels like a prison.

Q. Seems one of the most important things that we can do is to gather the Blue Diamond Souls together?

Yes, to allow us to find the support of one another, yes this is the ultimate experience for us, is to be around others like us to help us activate and remember who we are. It should not just be assumed that because we are this higher vibrational being, this advanced-intelligence Soul, it should not just be assumed that when we birth into your low density, three-dimensional body that we will necessarily remember immediately who we are. Part of your human condition is that as we come through the Soulstar, through in to the birth canal, there is much forgetting and this is part of your human condition. It is something that we are able to manage to some extent, yet also the environment that we are placed in will make a very big difference. If we are placed in an environment that shuts down the gifts of who we are, then it is highly likely that we will shut that down and that we will be forced into numbing and following the same path, but if we are brought through into a loving environment where we are able to express who we are, then we will remember very quickly. We will activate very quickly. But keep in mind that it is still possible to squash us by throwing us into all of your normal conditionings of numbing, because no matter how high vibration our Soul is, if we are trapped in a numb and vibrationally dead body, there is not much we can do to change that. So yes, placing us together helps us to remember who we are and helps us to grow into our higher intelligence quickly.

MESSAGES FROM THE BLUE DIAMOND SOULS

Q. What does the future hold for us?

There are many different possibilities that are remaining right now within the quantum field. So, this is highly dependent upon how quickly you as Humanity start to wake up. We are able to see a number of different paths that you may, as a Collective, unconsciously end up choosing. What we do see is that there will be a greater energy of fear and confusion that comes across the planet as people are being forced into waking up very rapidly. Some of you have been on this path of awakening for a long period of time, you have had the luxury of understanding and slowly processing what is shifting for you. Yet the masses will not have this luxury, you will be here to support the masses as they go into their inevitable crisis mode. However, that is where they are headed, that is almost a given, is that they must hit crisis point to see that there is another way, to see that they no longer wish to be controlled, that they no longer wish to be treated like they are in fact, stupid, and being manipulated and controlled by a small percentage of the population. And so as they wake up, you will see mass chaos in different parts of the planet.

Much of this will be driven by the human. Some of this will be driven by your atmosphere, by nature itself. Yet, this massive shakeup is precisely what is needed in

133

order to shift the direction of where you are all currently headed. Otherwise, the majority will continue to remain asleep and therefore you come to the end of Humanity. Therefore, you reach extinction.

Yet if we move through this time of crisis, and we understand that at times, chaos is needed, and, in fact, is what can create the magick of shift and of change. And we can approach that chaos with the energy and the vibrational frequency of Love, which is what we as Blue Diamond Souls hold. This is one of the reasons that we are birthing here now, is to be able to help you to hold this frequency of Love. If we can approach that chaos with love, then we foresee that one of the potential outcomes is to move through this quite quickly and to shift dimension and to completely change the way that you as humankind see your life. But there is a tipping point.

Because also we see the reality of a future where the fear remains and you cause your own demise. There is a choice. There is the option here of which way you as Humanity choose to go. You are at a point where you need to, each and every one of you, make a decision. Is it more important to you to remain controlled and manipulated and trapped in a way that you seem to feel safe, yet knowing that perhaps that will end in your eventual demise? Or is it more important to be in the discomfort of the now and the place that perhaps does not feel safe, yet is you waking up and shifting the direction of where humanity is headed and going to somewhere that is greater than what the majority of you can even imagine? This is your choice. We are here to support, without any judgement which direction you choose. We are here purely in service to show you that there is another way.

Q. And what can we do now as humans to look after this Earth?

You need to come together and to be one loud voice against the larger organisations who you have allowed to control you for all of these years, you need to now as Humanity move as one against these larger corporations who are doing everything they can to destroy the planet, to destroy the environment of the third dimension of where you live. Because, in fact, they are here intentionally to try to... I want to be careful of my words here to not instill more fear... but the intention of those in the higher corporations and organisations and governments, their heart is not pure.

We come with a vibration of Love. Their heart, to us, looks black. The intention of them is to continue to drive Humanity as fast as possible towards your own demise. This is part of their actual purpose here on earth. And so as Humanity, the more of you who can come together and move as one voice against what is happening, then this will ultimately lead to the breakdown of what they call leadership, which in actual fact is showing up in your reality as those who are in control and have the ability to manipulate and manage the masses.

If the masses are able to band together and realise that, rather than being the helpless one individual who is unable to stand up against a large corporation or government, that when they band together, actually this is the time that they can make a shift and they can make a change, then the more of these large corporations and organisations and governments are forced into a place of having to hand over their control of the human race. This is how you will begin to make rapid change on a planetary Earth level. As we've already spoken to plenty of times before, is that also the Love vibration and the frequency and shifting the vibrational frequency of the Earth, but to actually look directly to the physical plane of your earth, this is the most important step that you can take as humanity to ensure that you shift the path of where you are currently headed. What you need to also understand is that it only takes a micro degree of shift to start to make rapid change. It is not something to be looked at as a mammoth shift, that is not possible to be done. It literally can be as small as a micro shift, and the entire planetary path will shift into a different optional future, rather than one of your current trajectory, which, in the foreseeable future we see, is human destruction. Yet please don't allow yourself to be caught in the fear emotion of this, remembering that actually this is what the larger corporations, societies and governments have been doing to you is instilling fear in you to take away your power, so that you think that you think that you cannot make a change. Instead, we want you to shift away from the fear. Move into the experience of Love, band together as a Humanity moving as one Love vibration, that will shift everything as you currently know it because those in higher control at the moment, they do not hold this energy of Love. They only hold that of fear and of hate and that is what they have been spreading like a disease throughout your people. And now it is time to shift that and change that by bringing it into the heart to understand that it is a fight of Love. It is not a fight of fear and hate. This is the energy that has polarised you into the position that you are in. So instead of buying into the fear and the hate, we call you to band together because as your people you are able to love one another. We see this is where you can find the shift. You will see this happening in different countries throughout the world where there is natural, perhaps natural, perhaps

136

not natural, disasters. But there are disasters that are happening around your world that are banding people together, that are making people see that in actual fact if they move together as one that they are able to make a change.

Below the fear and the hate that may be expressed on the outside, this comes from a place of love. This comes from a place of supporting one another. You have people currently now in your world who are risking their own lives in order to save the houses and the lives of other people and other beings on your planet. They are doing this out of Love, they are doing this out of care for one another. This is the energy that needs to build. And so what we see is that disaster actually brings people to band together. And they band together in that place of Love, which we say can sometimes be hidden under the external fear. But if you look beneath what you will experience is Love.

For the human race to be moving more and more into this Love energy banding together and moving as one and bring that Love to those who are, who have been, controlling and manipulating with fear, the Love will always win over. This is what you as Humanity can be doing now to make rapid shift to what is happening to your planet, and to the atmosphere that you're currently living in.

Q. What are some of the most critical projects that need to be birthed?

There are many critical projects upon your Earth dimension right now that need to be birthed. And they are anything that is here to support human consciousness.

So, anything that is to support people to move out of their current state of fear energy, to release their past conditioning, release their past stories, to raise their own vibrational being, to understand that they are also a Soul instead of looking to their own life as if they are just one human without a greater higher purpose or a greater higher connection. So anything that is created with the highest of intent with the clearest of, find my words, anything that is created purely connected to Divine Will.

That is in service of Humanity, that which is not coming from a place of ego or a need to present something to the world, but it's coming from a place of a deep desire and a deep knowing that there is a difference to be made. There is a shift to be made in Humanity at this time, anything on a personal level. These projects are important. For example, organisations like Mystery Schools or Temple spaces or higher spiritual learning centres where people gather to support one another, for their own and the Collective, not only as the individual, these are of a high priority to us as projects that we may well support. Then on a greater, larger scale, anything that is here to shift the way that you as humankind are currently moving on this planet, anything that is to shift the destruction and the waste that is rapidly happening on this Earth. Anything that is to shift the vibrational frequency that is impacting the rape of the resources that you have, to be able to continue to survive on this planet. These are also extremely important projects, places that we would come to support. These are projects that are not for personal gain. These are projects that are not through mass corporation and personal financial gain. These are for only the betterment of the entire Collective. On an even larger, collective scale is any project that is being born to rapidly shift the frequency and the vibration that you all live upon. What we see and understand is that in a higher dimensional reality, that there are various technologies that allow us to shift and move the frequency rapidly. Yet it seems that so far, humankind are not moving on these technologies. And these are definitely projects that we are here to support, as this is where our intelligence lies as this is where we are truly able to guide and support Humanity, by bringing our understanding of 12th-dimensional technology into your three-dimensional realm. These are of extremely high importance, because as important as it is to continue to work on the personal and to look at each individual cell as part of the Collective, we will receive much faster transformation if we can change the technology of your Humanity.

Q. What advice do you have for Blue Diamond Souls on Earth who are reading this book?

This is very difficult because for us to communicate is not with words. Yet to form it into language, I tell them to remember. Remember who you are.

Remember where you came from. Know that you are not alone. There are many of us already here. Many already born in human form and many are already here within this dimension, and for you to remember that we are able to communicate without being able to see each other in physical form, to remember your own ways of where you came from.

And if you are finding it difficult here on earth to start to open your third eye and see the others, to gather together because there are many and as you already know, we are not many individuals. We are many expressions of the one organism.

Q. What is possible for Humanity through your help?

If humanity is able to raise the vibration of your Collective Womb and your people are able to continue to open the Portals for us and we are able to continue to conceive and birth into your dimension, the more of us that are able to arrive and to be nurtured, guided and supported as we go through the ease of childhood, until we are old enough to start to be able to work our mission, then the shifts that we are able to make on your planet for Humanity is to guide you safely away from possible extinction, extinction of the third-dimensional realm. And to be able to help you shift and guide as an entire Humanity together into the fifth-dimension. This, as we can see it from where we are, is the minimum of where you need to shift to in order to be able to really create a drastic change in Humanity as you know it.

We are not only different to you on a vibrational frequency, we come to you with a different DNA imprint, different DNA light code, perhaps it is not visual under your microscopes, yet it is very clear to us that our DNA light code is very different yours. And if we are able to shift you as Humanity, and then we are able to birth our own children, still Blue Diamond Souls but through us, through our own bodies, then this is where we can start to move into rapid ascension of Humanity.

When I keep saying you are at a pivotal time in, in your history, you are at a point where you are being offered great help. Yet you are also at a point where you have been fed much fear. And for many, it is very difficult to understand that there is another way other than this fear because it has been so well bred into you that this is the normal way of living, that this is the normal way of life.

And the closer you come to realising that humanity is heading in the direction of its own destruction, the more difficult it is for the human race to manage their own energy of fear and to shift that into the vibration of Love. So, it is like you are sitting at a pivotal point, and the more of you that can very quickly shift your energy and wake up and raise the vibration away from fear, the more likely it is that we are able to come in and make a rapid shift for Humanity. For for all of you, but it is not guaranteed at this point. We would like to be able to tell you that it is guaranteed, but it also requires your help. We have heard your call and we have arrived to help but you need to also help us to help you. We cannot change what is happening by ourselves. We need you to see that we are coming as your teachers and as your guides, and that we know the way and we need you to open and to listen to us, and to perhaps even help us be our voice.

So if you are a guardian to us, helping us find that voice and helping us share that voice with the world quicker. That will give us more opportunity to ensure that our mission here is completed in a timely manner and for the benefit of all.

Q. What do Blue Diamond Souls want from us?

For you to understand that for us to help you, we need you to help us. For you to understand that it is not all in the giving that you also must be open to giving in return. You must understand that if you desire our help, it may not be comfortable and that it will require you to change and it will require you to shift and it will require you to move through what feels extremely uncomfortable. It will require you to change your ways. It will require you to change your habits, to change your routine, to change

141

the way you act in the world. To change what you eat. It will require you to make massive change in your life. And so we ask of you to be open to this and we ask of you to understand that now is the time. In this time dimension, you have a way of wishing to put everything off. I will do it tomorrow, I should do that, I will do it tomorrow, I will do it next week. This is no longer an option. If you truly desire our help, then you need to do it. Now! Not to put something on your to-do list, to make a change later. But to make it your priority is to look at the state of the world and of Humanity right now. And rather than allowing the fear to overtake you, to shift that energy into your motivation to be able to know that you – even as one being you can make a change just by shifting your own reality and your own world, and that that will create its own ripple effect. Understanding that there is no point getting lost in the, "What can I do? It's only me," and instead diving into the understanding that it is YOU. There is so much you can do as one and you CAN impact the Collective.

Do everything you can to raise your vibration and to raise your frequency. Do everything you can to cut down and reduce the waste that you bring onto this planet. Do everything you can to shift the vibration of the Collective Womb to allow us to birth through you and do everything you can to listen to us, to support us and to guide us through the years that bring us into a place where we are able to complete our purpose and our mission.

Q. How can we support you better on your mission on Earth and and what is that mission?

Our mission is to lovingly support you as humankind, is to lovingly show you that there is another way, is to bring the energy of Love vibration, a different energy of Love than what many of you seem to be fooled into believing is Love. Love is not control and manipulation. Love is not to come from a place of fear. Love, in fact, is a vibrational frequency of freedom, of setting each heart in the world free to be open and realise that in actual fact, the truth of your being is Love. Yet we are here to help you wake up to see this reality. Because IF you are able to truly see this reality and start to move as Love in the world, then this is how you can make rapid change, is to start to live, "What would Love do in this moment? What would Love do in this situation?"

This is how you make rapid change because I foresee that not many of you, in your dimension, would believe that Love chooses to kill and destroy, that Love chooses to control and manipulate and turn people into mere robots rather than the alive beings and Souls that they are. So, the more of you that are able to move into this frequency and this understanding of what pure, Divine, "I Am" presence Love is, then there is no other way but to change the way you all move on the planet. We see that everything shifts with this vibration. So this is one of our purposes, is to guide you and to show you what this Love frequency is. One of our other purposes here is to support you with the technology, is to support you to start to awaken and understand that technology can be used for the raising of the vibration to shift and move through dimensions, as we have previously said. And to help you to see the way you have currently been using your technology to manipulate, control and put into 2D, that we can use that now to shift and focus you to raising the dimension, the frequency of your planet. We are here to wake you up. We are here to show that there is another way. Many of us will express this in different terms, in different actions, in how we move in the world. But when you are able to recognise who we are, choosing to support us in whatever it is that we foresee is able to support you as humankind, this will help support the greater. This will help support the collective. So, we see our purpose here with you is, as I say, the Love vibration, to guide you into what that is and to teach you how to live that. To help you understand how to shift your technology, also to start to wake you up to see what it is that you have currently been doing to your dimensional realm and this planet, and to support you in any way we possibly can. Much of that will be through environmental actions, to guide and to lead, especially as the majority of us are in bodies of children right now or very young adults.

We also see that adults are less likely, when they are confused, to attack with their words and their energy vibration, a small being who is holding the vibration of Love and who is holding the frequency of Innocence as they share their own pain and their own experience of the world with you. You are less likely to attack them with your words and with your energy than you are someone who you see as being an equal or lesser than you also in an adult form. So you will see more and more children and very young adults standing up in the world for environmental change and waking you up to see what in actual fact you have been allowing to happen to your planet, to your home. Because we believe that many of you actually do not even see what you have allowed because you have been so busy being caught and numbed or stuck in your two-dimensional technology that you have not even seen what is happening. It is like someone has come in and turned your house upside down. They have destroyed your house and they have taken everything of value from your house. But you were so busy watching the screen that you did not even notice. And suddenly the screen is turned off and you look up and your home is destroyed. This is where many of you are right now. And this is what these children are to help you to see, to turn off your two- dimensional screen and see what has happened to your home.

Q. How do you relate to our technology?

We are confused, that the things that you consider as technology tends to be a way to numb. Whereas for us technology is a way to continue to raise the frequency, change the vibrational reality, shift across dimensions, travel and move across dimensions with ease. Yet, much of your technology seems to be created to keep you focused on the inwards, to keep you focused on decreasing your vibrational frequency, to be a way to escape looking up to the reality of the world. We say that many of you spend your time trapped and caught in the technology as if you are a slave to it. As if somehow if you remain focused inside this small technology that it will either save you or that you will be able to disappear and hide in it, like as the demise of the world will happen, you may all be looking down staring at small screens. We find this a waste actually of what is possible with technology.

What we see is happening is that your government, your corporations, your large organisations, are very successfully using technology to train you, to enslave you, to trap you into a reality that blindsides you, that stops you from seeing what is truly happening in the world. Many of you are walking around stuck in this reality. In fact, we see that you are third- dimensional beings and that we are coming to help you shift as quickly as possible to at least five-dimensional beings, yet you use your technology

145

to convert you into two-dimensional beings, we find this confusing as for us, technology is for the opposite purpose. Technology for us is around raising our frequency, shifting to a higher dimension, knowing that there are much higher dimensions that we can reach, even in the 12th dimension that we are currently residing in, our use currently of technology is to take us to an even higher dimension than the 12th, this is what we work upon when it comes to technology. So, we are outwardly focused, you are inwardly focused with your technology. Yet much of what has been shared in your dimension around technology is also an important base, is also an important starting point. So those with the correct intelligence actually will be able to use what you have created so far in technology to then be able to shift and focus in the correct direction. Although we see so far that your technology has mostly been used for controlling you and for poisoning you along with habits we have spoken about before, the food and the water and the air that you breathe and the medications that you're given, that it is part of this turning you all into robots. We also see that, that technology gives us the start to move forward.

Yet, we need to be able to support you to see that on a greater Collective level. That way we can help you to shift your technology, to start to become a smaller carbon copy version of what it is that we can use on our dimension. And moving forward, it could be part of the saving grace of the third-dimensional being by bringing you into a higher dimension before you hit your own demise.

WANT MORE?

This book is an introduction to the depth of work that is available with Zapheria.

To find out more about her other offerings such as

The Womb Spiral
The Womb Spiral apprenticeship
The Womb Weavers mentoring program
The Cauldron membership
The Conscious Conception program
The Spiral

Head over to www.zapheriabell.com

And join the free Facebook women's group The Womb Weavers Collective

Make sure you claim your FREE book bonus material

- 18,000 words manuscript of unedited channelling directly from The Blue Diamond Souls

- Videos, meditations, rituals and audio's to further support all that you have read here

Visit www.zapheriabell.com/bookbonus

If this book hit a note for you and you want to join The Womb Weavers Collective as a practitioner The Womb Spiral Apprenticeship path may be for you. To receive an application form please email zapheria@zapheriabell.com and let Zapheria know why you feel called to this work.

For continued discussions on all things Blue Diamond Souls, Womb Activations, The Womb Gates, Conception, Birth, Pregnancy and Blue Diamond Soul children check out the Podcast at www.zapheriabell.com/podcast

After you read the book and the unedited transcription if you would like to ask The Blue Diamond Souls any questions to be included in any future books or answered on the podcast you can email bluediamondsouls@zapheriabell.com

CONTACTS & ACKNOWLEDGEMENTS

Throughout the book various mentors, processes and products were mentioned. Here are there details for you

The Spiral
www.thespiral.com

Clear Your Shit
www.clearyourshit.com

Dane Tomas
www.danetomas.com

Kundalini Dance
www.leyolahantara.com
www.kundalinidance.com

Janine MaRae
www.redearthtemple.com

Highden Mystery School
www.highdentemple.org

Crystal Synergy Ankh
www.cosmiccreations.com

GLOSSARY

Activated Womb
The energetic body of the Womb becoming active creates an activated womb

Altar
A place where offerings are placed for religious or spiritual purposes.

Amrita or Ambrosia
(Sanskrit) is often referred to in ancient Indian texts as nectar or the drink of the Gods. It is also the name for a women's ejaculate.

Auric Field
Subtle bodies create an interconnected field of energy around the physical body that is commonly known as the auric field .

Blue Diamond Souls
12th dimensional beings that are being born on Earth at this time in order to serve the rise in consciousness of humanity to the vibrational frequency of love.

Ceremony
A formal religious or spiritual occasion, an intentional community ritual of a spiritual nature

Cervix
The narrow passage forming the lower end of the uterus. The neck.

Channel

Serve as a medium for a spirit. To channel is to allow energy to flow through you. Just as water can be channeled, we can channel energy.

Chakra

An energetic center within and around the body that connects us to the world around us

Clitoris

The clitoris is the female's most sensitive erogenous zone. The head of the clitoris is a small, sensitive erectile part of the female genitalia at the anterior end of the vulva that contains 8000 nerve ending. The legs of the Clitoris wrap around and inside the labia.

Collective Womb

The womb that lives in the collective human psyche and energy field, the collective womb encompasses the Earth womb and the energetic wombs of all beings on the planet.

Conception

The action of conceiving a child or of one being conceived. The moment the egg is fertilised by the seed is the moment of conception.

Consciousness

The phenomena that allows us to perceive and have experience

Consciousness (scale of)

The Scale of consciousness is a scale that spans from 0-1000 rating the vibrational frequency of all things and emotions.

Conditioning

The process of training or accustoming a person to behave

in a certain way or to accept certain circumstances. 'Social Conditioning'. The patterns we create become part of our automatic behaviour.

Conscious conception
The art and practice of holding intention to invite a Soul/baby into your Womb.

Cosmic womb
The cosmic womb is the pregnant void of infinite possibilities and creativity. The feminine aspect of the Void.

Creation Point
The place where the Souls purpose is held and accessed. Also the 6th Gate of the Womb

Dimensions
The spiritual realm is defined as being/existence that is completely separated from the physical and mental realms and is divided into dimensions . Most people are used to the three dimensions we use to measure our reality. There are more dimensions available, some accessible to a few humans and some beyond our reach.

Divine
Of or like a God. Devoted to God, sacred.

Dogmatic
Dogma are rules and conventions. To be Dogmatic is to follow and enforce dogma even when it is not wise or working to do so.

Energy Field
The space created by a person or living beings energy that can create a magnetic or gravitational pull that is usually invisible but can often be sensed and felt.

Ecstasy

An overwhelming feeling of great happiness or joyful excitement. May also be the experience of ecstacy in the body as all cells begin to vibrate together.

Ecstatic Birth

Also called Orgasmic Birth. A phenomen of labor and delivery being pleasurable and of the body vibrating with ecstasy.

Ecstatic current

A vibrational current of the Earth that when tapped in to can provide the guidance and direction of where to move to next.

Etheric Womb

The etheric/energetic aspect of the Womb that lives within the energetic body of all living beings.

Fifth Dimension

The earth and all beings living on the planet are shifting into a whole new level of reality in which a consciousness of love, joy, peace, freedom, compassion and spiritual wisdom prevails . This has been called the Fifth Dimension.

Frequency

Energetically beings are vibrating at a certain frequency often associated with an emotion. Each of these emotions has a frequency that creates sensations in the body and emits energetic vibrations to everything around us.

Freeze

Become suddenly motionless or paralyzed with fear or shock of a person. This freeze may remain in the cells of the body for many years.

God Consciousness

An experience of Consciousness beyond Consciousness, connecting to the aspect of the Self that is able to transcend the human instincts. The seperation of the individual self and connection to the oneness of all that is.

G-Spot

A sensitive area of the anterior wall of the vagina that is capable of being highly erogenous and of stimulating ejaculation.

High Priestess

The chief female advocate or proponent of a particular belief or practice.

Humanity

Humanity is the human race, which includes everyone on earth.

Initiation

Is a rite of passage marking entrance or acceptance into a group, a society or a significant time in ones evolution.

ISTA

The International School of Temple Arts is an organization which facilitates workshops and tribal gatherings in the field of sexual shamanism, sexual healing and integrative attitudes towards mind, body, emotions, sexuality and shadow work

Kundalini Activations

Kundalini is your life force energy. It's believed that in those who are unawakened, their energy remains coiled at the base of their spine. For those who have an awakening event and become conscious, the energy spirals upwards, activating each chakra.

Kundalini Dance
A powerful, Shaminic healing journey through the chakras.

Light Codes
A code of light , a physical anchor point for light frequencies to be channeled through into our physical realm.

Light Grid
The light grid is a powerful matrix of sacred geometry forming an energetic grid which can be present in the human form and also lay within the Earth.

Lineage
Direct descent from an ancestor, ancestry or pedigree.

Longing
A yearning desire .

Love Frequency
About 528Hz. This frequency is the most significant of the ancient Solfeggio Frequencies. It has deep-rooted relationship with nature, and is present in everything. It also has mathematical significance and proven healing potential.
Also 500 on the scale of Consciousness Love is the tipping point for a new way of living.

Lemuria
The name of a " lost land" located in the Indian and pacific oceans. Accounts of Lemuria differ, but all share a common belief that a continent existed in ancient times and sank beneath the ocean as a result of a geological, often cataclysmic change, such as a pole shift.

Medium
Medium is a person who mediates communication between the spirit and the living realms.

Mentor
A person, esp. an experienced, person, who provides personal or professional guidance

Mystery School
A mystery school is a group of initiates who have dedicated themselves to preserving, protecting and perpetuating the mystery teachings, it is also a place to dedicate oneself to the Souls path.

Phallus
A Phallus is a penis (especially when erect)

Portal
An energetic opening between dimensions or realms that allows travel between the two.

Red Tent
The red tent is a place where women gather to honour their menstruation time either alone for reflection or together to share in the Magick of their moontime.

Ritual
A religious or solemn ceremony consisting of a series of actions performed according to a prescribed order.

Sacred Union
A sacred relationship is relationship in which we are inspired to see the Divine in another person. To experience oneness through the union of two.

Sacredness
Devoted or dedicated to a deity or to some religious or spiritual purpose; sacred music, sacred books, sacred altar objects or creating a space of sacredness.

Sarcophagus
A box like funeral receptacle typically adorned with a sculpture or inscription and associated with the ancient civilisations of Egypt, Rome and Greece.

Seed
In the context of this book seed is the sperm of a man.

Shakti
Shakti is the subtle energy that means "power" or "empowerment," the primordial cosmic energy, and represents the dynamic forces that are thought to move through the entire universe. Shakti embodies the active feminine energy of Shiva. Shakti is present in both men and women and in Taoism, shakti is known as chi.

Shamanic
Relating to the beliefs and practices associated with a shaman. Involves a practitioner teaching altered states of consciousness in order to perceive and interact with what they believe to be a spirit world and channel these transcendental energies into this world.

Shibari
A Japanese style of rope bondage that is considered an art form.

Soul
The spiritual or immaterial part of a human being

Soul midwife

A person who is able to guide an unborn Soul into the body at birth and also guide them out at the time of passing. A Soul Midwife may also assist people to find a deep connection to their own Soul in this lifetime.

Temple

A place dedicated to spiritual rituals, service or worship of a deity or deities and activities such as prayer.

The Spiral

The Spiral is a powerful process for clearing the emotional baggage and conditioning that stops us from expressing our true authentic selves.

The process was founded by Dane Tomas in 2012, and came together after 12 years of experimentation with different maps and models. It combines elements and learnings from Spiral Dynamics, Kinesiology, the Chakra System and The Scale of Consciousness.

The third dimension

A state of consciousness that is very limited and restricted. Third dimensional society and science seek to prove that the only reality that exists is the one we perceive with our five physical senses and urges us to believe that our 3D perceptions of reality are the only reality.

Transmission

The action or process of transmitting an energy, state or teaching from one person to another

The twelfth Dimension

Has a unified Field which means that when you work from this dimension, you simultaneously have access to the dimensions, magnetic, worlds and all aspects of the universe. The twelfth dimension resides outside of time and through (not in) space .

Vibration

Every action and every thought creates vibrations in the spiritual energy field, a person's emotional state, the atmosphere of a place, or the associations of an object, as communicated to and felt by others.

Womb

The organ in the lower body of a woman or female mammal where offspring are conceived and in which they gestate before birth, the uterus.

Womb Gates

7 energetic centres that travel from the vagina of a woman, through the womb and to the cosmic womb. Each gate is associated with an emotional gate key and creates a pathway to healing and activation of the womb.

Womb Spiral

Using the emotional clearing technique of The Spiral, the practitioner clears the emotions trapped in each Womb Gate which then opens the person up to experience more connection to their own bodies, more sensation and pleasure, more ease in conceiving and connects them to their own feminine power.

Yoni

The Sanskrit word for female genitals, translates to source or all life or sacred space.

NOTES

NOTES

NOTES

NOTES

NOTES

NOTES

NOTES

NOTES